Social Media Marketing Magic

Trends, Strategies, and Innovations to Dominate the Digital Space

Medina Fred

Copyright © 2025 by Medina Fred

All right reserved. No part of this book may be reproduced, stored in a retrieval system, or transmitted in any form or by any means, electronic, mechanical, photocopying, recording, or otherwise, without prior written permission from the author, except for brief quotations in critical reviews or articles.

Disclaimer

This book is designed to provide insights, strategies, and best practices in social media marketing. While every effort has been made to ensure accuracy, success depends on various factors, including personal effort, market conditions, and industry trends. The author and publisher are not responsible for individual outcomes. Readers are encouraged to adapt the strategies to their unique situations and seek professional advice when necessary.

Dedication

To the relentless innovators, digital pioneers, and every entrepreneur striving to make their mark in the digital space. This book is for those who dare to embrace change, challenge the status quo, and turn creativity into influence. Keep pushing boundaries—your voice matters.

Acknowledgment

Writing this book has been an incredible journey, and I couldn't have done it alone. I want to express my deepest gratitude to my mentors, colleagues, and the ever-evolving social media landscape that continues to inspire innovation.

A special thank you to my readers—whether you're an aspiring marketer, a seasoned strategist, or a business owner looking to amplify your online presence. Your passion for learning and growth is what drives this industry forward.

Lastly, to my family and close friends, your unwavering support and belief in me have made this journey even more rewarding. Thank you for being my constant source of inspiration.

TABLE OF CONTENTS

Dedication 3
Acknowledgment 4
INTRODUCTION 1
    Why Social Media Is Critical for Modern Businesses ... 1
    The Evolution of Social Media Marketing: Past to Present 2
    What Readers Will Gain 3
PART ONE 5
The Foundation of Social Media Marketing Success 5
CHAPTER 1: The Digital Landscape 7
    The State of Social Media in 2025 7
    The Role of Mobile, AI, and Emerging Technologies. 10
    Building a Strong Foundation for Social Media Success. 11
    Examples, Trends, and Tools for Success 13
CHAPTER 2: Defining Your Social Media Marketing Goals 14
    Identifying Objectives 14
    The Importance of KPIs and ROI Tracking 17
    Aligning Social Media Goals with Business Strategy .. 18
    Examples, Trends, and Tools for Defining Goals 20
CHAPTER 3: Crafting a Powerful Brand Identity 22
    Establishing a Distinct Brand Voice 22
    Creating Consistent Visual Branding 24
    Building Trust and Credibility in a Digital World 26
        Examples, Trends, and Tools for Building Brand Identity 27
PART TWO 30

Strategies for Engaging Content and Growth................30

CHAPTER 4: Content Creation That Converts............32

    The Power of Storytelling... 32

    Formats That Work: Videos, Reels, Stories, and Posts 34

    Designing Shareable and Viral Content...................... 36

    Leveraging User-Generated Content (UGC).............37

    Interactive Technologies: Fostering Deeper Connections 38

CHAPTER 5: The Magic of Interactive and Immersive Content..40

    Using Augmented Reality (AR) for Campaigns.......... 40

    Polls, Quizzes, and Live Sessions for Engagement......42

    Creating Personalized Experiences with AI................ 44

    Integrating Interactive and Immersive Content into Your Strategy..46

CHAPTER 6: Harnessing User-Generated Content (UGC).. 48

    Encouraging and Showcasing UGC.......................... 48

    Building Community Loyalty Through Involvement.. 50

    Leveraging Influencers and Brand Ambassadors.........52

    Integrating UGC into Your Broader Strategy...............54

PART THREE.. 56

Platform-Specific Strategies..56

CHAPTER 7: Dominating Facebook and Instagram....58

    Understanding Facebook and Instagram Features and Demographics..58

    Using Facebook Groups for Community Building...... 59

    Shopping Features and Ads on Instagram...................61

    Trends in Visual and Short-Form Content...................62

Staying Ahead of Platform-Specific Trends................64

CHAPTER 8: Cracking the Code of TikTok and Emerging Platforms..**66**

Understanding TikTok and Emerging Platforms..........66

Creating Engaging, Trendy, and Authentic Videos......67

Leveraging TikTok for Brand Awareness and Conversions..69

Keeping an Eye on New Emerging Platforms..............70

Staying Ahead of Trends...72

CHAPTER 9: LinkedIn and Twitter/X for Thought Leadership..**74**

Using LinkedIn for B2B Networking and Lead Generation..74

Twitter/X for Real-Time Marketing and Engagement. 76

Campaign:..78

Result:..78

Staying Ahead of Trends and Algorithms.....................79

PART FOUR..**81**

Advanced Strategies and Innovations.......................**81**

CHAPTER 10: The Role of AI in Social Media Marketing...**83**

AI-Driven Content Creation Tools................................83

Predictive Analytics for Campaign Planning................84

Chatbots for Instant Engagement.................................86

Integrating AI, AR, and Blockchain for Future Success..87

Tips for Staying Ahead of Competitors........................88

CHAPTER 11: Paid Advertising Mastery.....................**90**

Advanced Targeting Strategies.....................................90

Creating High-Converting Ad Campaigns................92
Measuring Success with Performance Metrics........... 94
Leveraging Innovative Technologies in Paid Advertising... 95
Tips for Optimizing Paid Advertising ROI................. 96

CHAPTER 12: Leveraging Influencer Partnerships.... 98
Finding the Right Influencers for Your Brand............ 98
Building Long-Term Relationships............................ 100
Measuring the ROI of Influencer Campaigns........... 102
Integrating Innovation into Influencer Partnerships...103
Tips for Scaling Influencer Campaigns..................... 104

PART FIVE... 106
Measuring Success and Continuous Improvement......106
Why Continuous Improvement Matters..................... 108
What to Expect in This Part....................................... 108

CHAPTER 13: Data-Driven Decision Making............110
Essential Social Media Analytics Tools..................... 110
How to Interpret and Act on Insights........................ 112
Tracking Trends Over Time.......................................113
The Importance of A/B Testing................................. 115
Practical Tools for Tracking and Refinement............ 116

CHAPTER 14: A/B Testing and Optimization............118
Testing Content, Ads, and Campaigns...................... 118
Implementing Changes Based on Results.................. 120
Staying Agile in a Rapidly Changing Environment... 121
Practical Examples and Tools for Optimization......... 122
The Importance of Continuous Improvement............ 123

PART SIX... 125
Preparing for the Future... 125

    The Impact of Emerging Technologies................ 126
    Sustainability and Ethical Marketing................... 128
    The Importance of Adaptability and Agility......... 129

CHAPTER 15: Emerging Trends in Social Media Marketing.. 131
    The Rise of Decentralized Social Media.................... 131
    The Future of AR/VR in Social Media...................... 133

CHAPTER 16: Adapting to a Dynamic Digital Landscape.. 137
    How to Stay Ahead of Algorithm Changes................ 137
    Tools and Resources for Lifelong Learning............... 139
    Building Resilience for Long-Term Success............. 141

CONCLUSION.. 146
Turning Magic Into Mastery...146
    Recap of Key Insights and Takeaways...................... 146
    Applying the Magic to Your Brand............................ 148
    Encouragement to Innovate, Adapt, and Lead........... 148

INTRODUCTION

Social media has transformed the way businesses connect with their audiences. What began as platforms for sharing personal updates and photos has evolved into a powerful ecosystem that drives global commerce, builds communities, and creates opportunities for businesses of all sizes. In today's digital-first world, mastering social media is not optional—it's essential for businesses that aim to stay competitive, grow, and dominate their markets. However, the ever-changing landscape of social media can feel overwhelming. Algorithms shift, new platforms emerge, and audience behaviors evolve faster than ever. Many businesses struggle to keep up, while others miss opportunities by relying on outdated strategies. This book is here to change that.

By taking a holistic approach to social media marketing—blending cutting-edge trends, actionable strategies, and forward-thinking innovations—this book will equip you with the tools and insights to not just survive but thrive in the digital space. Let's dive into why social media is critical for modern businesses and what makes this book your ultimate guide to navigating and succeeding in this dynamic environment.

Why Social Media Is Critical for Modern Businesses

Social media is no longer just a marketing tool; it's a business necessity. With billions of users logging into platforms daily, social media offers unparalleled access to potential customers.

Unlike traditional advertising, social media provides a two-way channel where businesses can interact directly with their audience, building trust and fostering loyalty.

Key reasons social media is indispensable for modern businesses include:

1. **Reach and Scale:** Platforms like Instagram, TikTok, and LinkedIn allow businesses to reach global audiences, regardless of size or industry.
2. **Targeted Marketing:** Advanced algorithms and analytics enable hyper-specific targeting, ensuring your content reaches the right people at the right time.
3. **Cost-Effective Advertising:** Social media ads often yield higher returns on investment than traditional advertising methods.
4. **Community Building:** Social media fosters direct connections with customers, creating a sense of community and brand loyalty.

Whether you're a startup looking to establish a presence or an established company aiming to expand, social media is the bridge to your audience and the key to sustained growth.

The Evolution of Social Media Marketing: Past to Present

The journey of social media marketing is one of constant innovation. In the early 2000s, platforms like MySpace and Facebook introduced the concept of digital communities. Marketing on these platforms was straightforward—post an update, and your entire audience would see it.

Fast forward to today, and the landscape is unrecognizable. Algorithms prioritize meaningful engagement over simple reach. Short-form video dominates, and platforms like TikTok and Instagram Stories have redefined how brands capture attention. At the same time, advanced analytics and AI-driven tools have revolutionized how marketers measure success and tailor strategies.

Understanding this evolution is critical because it highlights the need to stay agile and adaptive. What worked five years ago may no longer be effective, and businesses that fail to innovate risk falling behind.

What Makes This Book Different

A Holistic Approach to Trends, Strategies, and Innovations: This book is not just another guide to social media marketing. While many resources focus on individual strategies or platforms, this book takes a holistic approach. It examines the entire ecosystem—how trends, strategies, and innovations work together to create powerful marketing opportunities.

You'll learn not only how to leverage existing platforms but also how to prepare for the future of social media marketing. From harnessing AI and automation to embracing ethical practices and emerging technologies, this book equips you with a complete toolkit for success.

What Readers Will Gain

Practical Tools, Insights, and Future-Proof Strategies

By the end of this book, you'll have a comprehensive understanding of social media marketing and the confidence to implement strategies that work. Specifically, you will:

- **Master Platform-Specific Strategies:** Learn how to dominate on platforms like Instagram, TikTok, LinkedIn, and beyond.
- **Stay Ahead of Trends:** Understand emerging technologies and how they'll shape the future of marketing.
- **Build Long-Term Success:** Develop a sustainable social media strategy that adapts to changing times.

Whether you're a seasoned marketer or just beginning your journey, this book will serve as your blueprint for mastering the art and science of social media marketing. Let's unlock the magic together.

PART ONE

The Foundation of Social Media Marketing Success

Social media marketing is a dynamic and ever-evolving field, but the principles of success remain rooted in a strong foundation. Without clear goals, a well-defined brand identity, and a solid understanding of the digital landscape, businesses risk being swept away in the tide of endless competition.

In this section, we'll lay the groundwork for your social media marketing journey. Whether you're a seasoned marketer or a beginner, establishing the right fundamentals is key to achieving sustainable growth and meaningful engagement in the digital space.

We'll begin by exploring the digital landscape as it stands today, understanding the platforms and technologies shaping the future of social media marketing. Next, we'll dive into the critical importance of goal-setting, outlining how to align your social media efforts with overarching business strategies. Finally, we'll uncover the secrets to crafting a powerful brand identity—one that resonates with your audience and sets you apart from the crowd.

CHAPTER 1: The Digital Landscape

Social media marketing has evolved into one of the most impactful tools for businesses to connect with their audiences, build brand loyalty, and drive sales. As we look ahead to 2025, the landscape continues to shift, driven by technological advancements, changing consumer behaviors, and the emergence of new platforms.

To succeed in this dynamic environment, businesses must deeply understand the state of social media, its most influential platforms, and the technologies shaping its future. This chapter provides the foundational knowledge and strategies needed to establish a strong presence in the ever-evolving digital landscape.

The State of Social Media in 2025

Unprecedented Global Reach

As of 2024, social media boasts over 5 billion users worldwide, making it one of the most ubiquitous digital tools. Platforms are no longer confined to specific age groups or demographics; instead, they cater to diverse global audiences with varying interests and behaviors.

- **Facebook and Instagram** continue to dominate in terms of active users, with features tailored for community building and e-commerce.

- **TikTok** remains a cultural phenomenon, capturing Gen Z and Millennial audiences through short-form video content.
- **LinkedIn** has solidified its role as the go-to platform for B2B marketing and professional networking.

Changing User Behaviors

In 2025, users demand:

- **Authenticity:** Audiences prefer brands that are transparent and relatable.
- **Interactive Experiences:** Features like live videos, polls, and augmented reality filters engage users more effectively.
- **Privacy and Control:** With increased awareness of data privacy, users gravitate toward platforms that prioritize ethical data practices.

Emerging Trends

- **Short-Form Video Dominance:** Platforms like TikTok, YouTube Shorts, and Instagram Reels continue to thrive.
- **Decentralized Platforms:** The rise of blockchain-based social networks offers users more control over their data.
- **Social Commerce Integration:** Shoppable posts and in-app purchases make it easier for users to transition from browsing to buying.

Key Platforms and Their Unique Audiences

Facebook

- **Audience:** Broad demographic appeal, particularly for users aged 25–55.
- **Strengths:** Community-building features like groups and events, paired with robust ad targeting options.
- **Best Uses:** Building brand awareness, engaging communities, and running targeted ad campaigns.

Instagram

- **Audience:** Visual-first platform with a strong Millennial and Gen Z presence.
- **Strengths:** Shoppable posts, Stories, and Reels for engaging, visually appealing content.
- **Best Uses:** Showcasing products, leveraging influencers, and storytelling.

TikTok

- **Audience:** Primarily Gen Z and Millennials, with increasing adoption among older demographics.
- **Strengths:** Viral potential and trend-driven content.
- **Best Uses:** Creative storytelling, brand challenges, and authentic audience engagement.

LinkedIn

- **Audience:** Professionals and businesses; ideal for B2B marketing.
- **Strengths:** Thought leadership and networking opportunities.

- **Best Uses:** Sharing insights, building credibility, and generating leads.

Emerging Platforms

- Keep an eye on **decentralized networks** like Mastodon and **AI-driven platforms** that customize content feeds for individual users.

The Role of Mobile, AI, and Emerging Technologies

Mobile Dominance

- **Fact:** Over 90% of social media usage happens on mobile devices.
- Businesses must prioritize **mobile-friendly content**, such as vertical videos, concise captions, and responsive design for ads.
- **Mobile Apps:** Advanced apps offer analytics, scheduling, and real-time engagement tools to streamline marketing efforts.

AI in Social Media Marketing

AI has revolutionized how businesses approach social media.

- **Content Creation:** Tools like ChatGPT assist with generating captions, blog posts, and ad copy.

- **Analytics and Insights:** AI-driven platforms analyze user data to predict trends and optimize campaigns.
- **Customer Engagement:** Chatbots powered by AI provide instant responses to customer queries, enhancing user experience.

Emerging Technologies

- **Augmented Reality (AR):** Brands use AR for interactive campaigns, such as virtual try-ons or immersive ads.
- **Blockchain:** Decentralized networks offer greater transparency and data security.
- **Voice and Visual Search:** Platforms now support searching via images or voice commands, changing how users discover content.

Building a Strong Foundation for Social Media Success

Defining Clear Goals

Every successful social media strategy begins with clear, measurable goals.

- **Brand Awareness:** Expand your reach and introduce your brand to new audiences.

- **Engagement:** Build meaningful connections through comments, shares, and interactions.
- **Lead Generation and Sales:** Use ads and shoppable posts to convert followers into customers.
- **Customer Support:** Provide fast, reliable assistance to maintain customer satisfaction.

Building a Brand Identity

- **Consistency is Key:** Use consistent logos, color schemes, and tone across platforms.
- **Define Your Voice:** Is your brand professional, playful, or inspirational? Tailor your messaging accordingly.
- **Engage Authentically:** Share behind-the-scenes content and respond to comments to humanize your brand.

Aligning Marketing Efforts with Business Objectives

Social media should complement your overall business strategy.

- **Integration:** Ensure your campaigns align with email marketing, content marketing, and offline initiatives.
- **Cross-Promotion:** Use social media to drive traffic to your website or other channels.
- **Team Collaboration:** Marketing, sales, and customer service teams should work together to provide a seamless customer experience.

Examples, Trends, and Tools for Success

Examples

1. **Case Study: Nike**
   Nike leverages Instagram Stories and TikTok challenges to engage younger audiences while maintaining a strong brand identity.
2. **Case Study: Starbucks**
   Starbucks uses Twitter and Instagram to build customer loyalty through user-generated content and promotions.

Trends to Watch

1. **Interactive Polls and Quizzes:** Boost engagement by encouraging audience participation.
2. **Ephemeral Content:** Temporary posts, like Stories, drive urgency and frequent interactions.

Tools for Success

1. **Hootsuite and Buffer:** For scheduling posts and tracking performance.
2. **Canva:** For creating visually appealing content.
3. **Google Analytics:** To measure traffic driven by social media.
4. **Sprout Social:** For advanced analytics and audience insights.

CHAPTER 2: Defining Your Social Media Marketing Goals

The success of any social media marketing strategy begins with clearly defined goals. Without a roadmap, it's easy to waste time and resources on campaigns that don't drive meaningful results. This chapter will guide you through the process of identifying objectives, tracking performance, and ensuring that your social media efforts align with broader business goals.

Identifying Objectives

Your goals on social media will depend on your business's overall objectives. Most companies focus on four primary areas: **awareness, engagement, leads, and sales.**

1. **Awareness: Building Your Brand's Presence**

    - **Definition:** Increasing the visibility of your brand and reaching new audiences.
    - **Why It Matters:** Awareness is the first step in the customer journey. Before customers can buy from you, they need to know you exist.
    - **How to Achieve It:**
        o Use paid ads and boosted posts to reach a larger audience.
        o Leverage influencers or partnerships to introduce your brand to their followers.

- - Create shareable content, such as memes or viral videos, to expand your reach organically.
  - **Example:** A local bakery posts mouth-watering images of their products on Instagram, using trending hashtags to attract food lovers in their area.

2. **Engagement: Connecting with Your Audience**

   - **Definition:** Encouraging interactions, such as likes, comments, shares, and direct messages.
   - **Why It Matters:** Engagement builds relationships and fosters community, increasing loyalty and retention.
   - **How to Achieve It:**
     - Post content that invites participation, such as polls, quizzes, or questions.
     - Respond promptly to comments and messages to show your audience you value them.
     - Host live events, webinars, or Q&A sessions to interact in real-time.
   - **Example:** A fitness influencer runs weekly Instagram Lives where followers can ask workout-related questions and share their progress.

3. **Leads: Capturing Potential Customers**

   - **Definition:** Generating interest from potential customers who may eventually purchase your product or service.

- **Why It Matters:** Leads bridge the gap between awareness and sales, creating a pool of prospects to nurture.
- **How to Achieve It:**
    - Offer downloadable resources like eBooks or templates in exchange for email sign-ups.
    - Use lead-generation ads on platforms like Facebook and LinkedIn.
    - Run contests or giveaways that require participants to provide their contact information.
- **Example:** A SaaS company offers a free trial for their software, promoted through LinkedIn lead-gen ads.

4. **Sales: Driving Revenue Through Social Media**

- **Definition:** Converting followers and leads into paying customers.
- **Why It Matters:** Sales are the ultimate measure of success for most businesses.
- **How to Achieve It:**
    - Use shoppable posts and product tags on platforms like Instagram and Pinterest.
    - Share customer testimonials or case studies to build trust and encourage conversions.
    - Retarget users who have interacted with your website or ads but haven't made a purchase.
- **Example:** An online clothing retailer uses Facebook ads to retarget users who abandoned their shopping cart.

The Importance of KPIs and ROI Tracking

Once your goals are defined, tracking performance through key performance indicators (KPIs) and return on investment (ROI) becomes essential.

1. Understanding KPIs

- **Definition:** KPIs are measurable values that indicate the success of your social media efforts.
- **Choosing the Right KPIs:**
    - For Awareness: Impressions, reach, and follower growth.
    - For Engagement: Likes, shares, comments, and video views.
    - For Leads: Click-through rates (CTR), form submissions, and sign-ups.
    - For Sales: Conversion rates, revenue generated, and cost per acquisition (CPA).
- **Example:** A travel agency uses CTR and bookings from Instagram ads to gauge campaign success.

2. Tracking ROI

- **Definition:** ROI measures the profitability of your social media investments.
- **How to Calculate ROI:**

- o **Formula:** (Revenue from Social Media − Costs of Social Media) ÷ Costs of Social Media × 100.
  - o Include costs such as ad spend, software, and time spent on content creation.
- **Tips for Maximizing ROI:**
  - o Focus on high-performing platforms that deliver the best results.
  - o Continuously optimize campaigns based on data insights.
- **Example:** An eCommerce brand spends $1,000 on Facebook ads and earns $5,000 in sales, achieving an ROI of 400%.

Tools for Tracking KPIs and ROI

1. **Google Analytics:** Tracks website traffic and conversions from social media.
2. **Sprout Social:** Monitors engagement and audience insights.
3. **HubSpot:** Measures lead generation and ROI across platforms.

Aligning Social Media Goals with Business Strategy

To maximize the impact of social media, your goals must align with your overarching business objectives.

1. **Integrating Social Media into Business Goals**

   - **Example Objective:** A company wants to increase its market share by 10%.
   - **Aligned Social Media Goal:** Build brand awareness among untapped demographics through targeted ads.

2. **Prioritizing Goals Based on Business Needs**

   - **Startups:** Focus on awareness and engagement to build a loyal following.
   - **Established Businesses:** Shift to lead generation and sales to drive revenue growth.
   - **Nonprofits:** Emphasize awareness and engagement to amplify their mission.

3. **Cross-Functional Collaboration**

   - **Marketing and Sales:** Ensure social media campaigns align with sales targets.
   - **Customer Service:** Use social media as a channel for responding to customer queries.
   - **HR and Recruitment:** Leverage LinkedIn to attract top talent.

4. **Creating a Unified Brand Message**

   - Maintain consistency across all marketing channels.
   - Use a cohesive tone of voice and visual identity to strengthen brand recognition.
   - Ensure all social media efforts contribute to the company's broader mission and values.

Examples, Trends, and Tools for Defining Goals

Examples

- **Case Study: Glossier**
  Glossier's focus on engagement has built a cult following. Their Instagram strategy emphasizes community interaction, turning followers into loyal customers.
- **Case Study: Airbnb**
  Airbnb's awareness campaigns showcase user-generated content, inspiring travelers and reinforcing their brand mission of belonging.

Trends to Watch

- **Purpose-Driven Marketing:** Consumers increasingly favor brands with clear missions and values.
- **Interactive Features:** Use tools like quizzes, polls, and live streams to enhance engagement.
- **Personalization:** AI-driven tools can tailor content to individual preferences, boosting relevance and impact.

Tools for Success

1. **Trello or Asana:** For setting and tracking goals.

2. **Google Data Studio:** For visualizing KPIs in real time.
3. **Canva:** To create content aligned with branding goals.

Defining clear social media marketing goals is the cornerstone of any successful strategy. By identifying objectives such as awareness, engagement, leads, and sales, and aligning these goals with your broader business strategy, you can create a roadmap for achieving meaningful results.

With the right KPIs, ROI tracking, and actionable insights, you'll be equipped to navigate the dynamic social media landscape with confidence and purpose. Remember, clarity in your goals today paves the way for success tomorrow.

CHAPTER 3: Crafting a Powerful Brand Identity

A strong brand identity is the cornerstone of social media marketing success. In today's digital world, where users encounter countless brands daily, standing out requires a cohesive and compelling identity that resonates with your audience. This chapter delves into how to establish a distinct brand voice, create consistent visual branding, and build trust and credibility in the ever-competitive digital landscape.

Establishing a Distinct Brand Voice

Your brand voice is the personality and tone conveyed in your communications. It reflects your values, resonates with your audience, and differentiates you from competitors.

1. Understanding Brand Voice

- **Definition:** Brand voice is the unique way your brand communicates, encompassing tone, language, and style.
- **Why It Matters:** A clear voice helps foster connection, trust, and recognition, making your brand memorable.
- **Examples of Brand Voices:**
    - **Playful and Fun:** Wendy's on Twitter uses humor and wit to engage audiences.

- **Professional and Authoritative:** IBM maintains a serious, knowledge-driven tone on LinkedIn.
- **Inspirational and Aspirational:** Nike's voice motivates and uplifts its audience.

2. Steps to Define Your Brand Voice

a. Identify Your Core Values

What principles define your business? For example:

- **Authenticity:** Show transparency and relatability.
- **Innovation:** Highlight cutting-edge solutions.
- **Empathy:** Demonstrate understanding and care for your audience's needs.

b. Understand Your Target Audience

- Consider age, preferences, challenges, and aspirations.
- Match your tone to the platform (e.g., casual on Instagram, formal on LinkedIn).

c. Document Your Voice Guidelines

Create a voice and tone guide that outlines:

- **Word Choices:** Formal vs. informal, complex vs. simple language.
- **Tone Adjustments:** Friendly for social posts, serious for industry whitepapers.

- **Dos and Don'ts:** Avoid slang or technical jargon, depending on your audience.

Creating Consistent Visual Branding

In the fast-paced world of social media, your visuals often make the first impression. Consistency in visual branding reinforces recognition, fosters trust, and amplifies your messaging.

1. Components of Visual Branding

a. Logo and Typography

- Ensure your logo is adaptable for all platforms (e.g., profile pictures, cover images).
- Use consistent fonts for posts, ads, and videos.

b. Color Palette

- Choose 3-5 primary colors that align with your brand personality.
- **Example:** Coca-Cola's red evokes excitement and passion, while Tiffany & Co.'s blue conveys luxury and sophistication.

c. Imagery and Graphics

- Use high-quality images that align with your tone.

- Incorporate branded graphics, like watermarks or overlays, in posts.

d. Templates and Layouts

- Create templates for social posts, ensuring consistency across campaigns.
- Use tools like Canva or Adobe Spark for design simplicity.

2. Maintaining Consistency Across Platforms

- Adapt content to platform requirements while retaining brand elements.
    - **Example:** Use vertical videos for Instagram Reels but keep colors and logos consistent.
- Ensure profile pictures, cover photos, and bios match your brand identity.

3. Tools for Visual Branding

1. **Canva:** Create templates for posts and presentations.
2. **Adobe Suite:** For advanced graphic design.
3. **Tailwind:** To manage Instagram and Pinterest aesthetics.

Building Trust and Credibility in a Digital World

In an age of information overload, trust is the foundation of successful relationships with your audience. Building credibility ensures that customers not only engage with your brand but also remain loyal to it.

1. The Importance of Trust in Social Media Marketing

- **Fact:** 81% of consumers say trust influences their buying decisions.
- **Trust Signals:** Positive reviews, user-generated content, and transparency strengthen your reputation.

2. Strategies for Building Trust

a. Transparency

- Be open about your business practices, pricing, and policies.
- Share behind-the-scenes content to humanize your brand.
    - **Example:** A local coffee shop posts stories showing how their beans are sourced ethically.

b. Consistent and Authentic Engagement

- Respond promptly and sincerely to comments, questions, and messages.

- Use a tone that feels genuine rather than overly sales-driven.
    - **Example:** An eco-friendly skincare brand posts stories answering FAQs with sincerity.

c. Social Proof

- Share testimonials, reviews, and case studies.
- Highlight user-generated content that showcases real customer experiences.
    - **Example:** A fitness brand reposts transformation photos from satisfied customers.

d. Influencer Partnerships

- Collaborate with trusted influencers who align with your values and audience.
    - **Example:** A sustainable fashion brand partners with eco-conscious influencers to promote their new collection.

e. Consistent Quality

- Ensure your content, products, and services meet or exceed customer expectations.
- Regularly update your audience on improvements or innovations.

Examples, Trends, and Tools for Building Brand Identity

Examples

1. **Apple:** Maintains minimalistic visuals and a tone of innovation, setting a benchmark for branding consistency.
2. **Lush Cosmetics:** Combines bold visuals with a conversational voice to promote its eco-friendly mission.

Trends

1. **Authenticity Over Perfection:** Audiences prefer relatable content, even if it's less polished.
2. **Personalization:** Brands that address users by name or tailor content to their preferences build stronger connections.
3. **Storytelling:** Narratives that align with brand values captivate audiences and drive engagement.

Tools for Success

1. **Brand Kit (Canva Pro):** Store logos, fonts, and colors for seamless content creation.
2. **Hootsuite or Buffer:** Schedule consistent posts across platforms.
3. **BuzzSumo:** Identify trending topics and influencers that align with your brand.

Crafting a powerful brand identity is essential for success in social media marketing. By establishing a distinct voice, creating consistent visuals, and prioritizing trust, you can create a brand that resonates deeply with your audience.

Remember, your brand identity is not just about how you look or sound; it's about how you make your audience feel. Invest time in refining your voice, visuals, and credibility to build lasting relationships that drive loyalty and growth in the ever-evolving digital world.

PART TWO

Strategies for Engaging Content and Growth

Content is the lifeblood of social media marketing. It's what attracts, engages, and retains your audience, and it's the foundation upon which successful brands build their communities. But creating content that resonates deeply with your audience and drives measurable growth is both an art and a science.

In this section, we'll explore the strategies behind crafting compelling, value-driven content and leveraging it to foster growth. From mastering the art of storytelling to incorporating the latest trends and technologies, this part of the book will equip you with actionable techniques to stand out in the crowded social media landscape.

We'll also delve into the nuances of audience engagement—how to spark meaningful conversations, foster loyalty, and turn followers into brand advocates. Growth isn't just about gaining followers; it's about cultivating a community that is invested in your brand's journey.

By the end of this section, you'll have a toolkit of proven strategies to create impactful content and achieve sustainable growth. Whether you're looking to go viral or build a niche, engaged audience, these chapters will provide the guidance you need to succeed. Let's uncover the secrets to engaging content and exponential growth

CHAPTER 4: Content Creation That Converts

Creating content that not only grabs attention but also drives meaningful action is the ultimate goal of social media marketing. In a digital ecosystem saturated with noise, the ability to craft compelling, shareable, and actionable content is what separates thriving brands from the rest.

This chapter will guide you through the essential techniques and strategies for designing content that converts. From harnessing the power of storytelling to mastering effective formats like videos and reels, you'll learn how to captivate your audience and inspire them to engage. We'll also explore how to leverage user-generated content, interactive technologies, and the psychology behind viral success to amplify your reach and impact.

The Power of Storytelling

Storytelling is at the heart of human connection, and it's one of the most powerful tools in a marketer's arsenal. When done right, stories can evoke emotions, build trust, and inspire action.

1. Why Storytelling Matters

- **Emotional Connection:** Stories resonate with audiences on a personal level, fostering trust and loyalty.

- **Memorability:** People remember stories far better than they remember facts or statistics.
- **Differentiation:** In a crowded market, a compelling narrative helps your brand stand out.

2. Crafting a Story That Converts

a. Know Your Audience

- Understand their pain points, aspirations, and values.
- Tailor your story to address their specific needs.
  - **Example:** A fitness brand shares transformation stories of individuals who overcame challenges to inspire others.

b. Follow a Story Arc

- **Introduction:** Present a relatable problem or scenario.
- **Climax:** Showcase your brand, product, or service as the solution.
- **Resolution:** Highlight the positive outcome, leaving the audience inspired and ready to act.
  - **Example:** A coffee brand narrates the journey of how it's ethically sourced beans support farmers and provide premium coffee for consumers.

c. Use Visual and Emotional Triggers

- Incorporate striking visuals, relatable characters, and evocative language to create a lasting impression.

Formats That Work: Videos, Reels, Stories, and Posts

Different content formats serve different purposes, and understanding their strengths is key to maximizing engagement.

1. The Rise of Video Content

a. Why Video is Dominant

- Videos are engaging, versatile, and highly shareable.
- Platforms like TikTok, Instagram, and YouTube prioritize video content in their algorithms.
  - **Fact:** Video posts get 48% more views than non-video posts on average.

b. Creating Effective Videos

- Keep them **short and impactful** (under 60 seconds for maximum engagement).
- Focus on storytelling, humor, or education.
- Add captions for accessibility and increased retention.

c. Tools for Video Creation

- **CapCut:** For editing short-form videos.
- **Canva:** For creating animated graphics.
- **Final Cut Pro:** For advanced editing.

2. Mastering Reels and Stories

a. Why They Work

- Bite-sized, ephemeral content encourages quick consumption.
- Stories create FOMO (fear of missing out) due to their limited availability.

b. Tips for Reels and Stories

- Use trending audio to increase discoverability.
- Incorporate interactive elements like polls, questions, or swipe-up links.
- Highlight customer testimonials or behind-the-scenes content for authenticity.

3. Optimizing Posts for Engagement

a. Static Images

- Use eye-catching visuals with bold headlines or quotes.
- Add a call-to-action (CTA) to encourage comments, shares, or clicks.

b. Carousels

- Share step-by-step guides, infographics, or product features.
- Use the first slide to hook viewers with a compelling question or statement.

Designing Shareable and Viral Content

While there's no guaranteed formula for virality, there are strategies to increase the likelihood of your content being widely shared.

1. Characteristics of Shareable Content

- **Relatable:** Speaks to universal emotions or experiences.
- **Entertaining:** Funny, surprising, or visually stunning.
- **Informative:** Offers value through tips, hacks, or insights.

2. Strategies for Creating Viral Content

a. Focus on Trends

- Monitor trending topics, hashtags, and formats on platforms like TikTok and Instagram.
- Adapt trends to align with your brand identity.
    - **Example:** A skincare brand participates in a popular "before-and-after" trend to showcase product effectiveness.

b. Encourage User Participation

- Create challenges or prompts that inspire your audience to generate content.

- **Example:** A coffee brand starts a "Latte Art Challenge" and features submissions on its page.

c. Optimize for Sharing

- Include CTAs like "Tag a friend" or "Share this if you agree."
- Ensure your branding is visible but not intrusive.

Leveraging User-Generated Content (UGC)

User-generated content is one of the most authentic and cost-effective ways to engage your audience and build trust.

1. Why UGC Matters

- **Authenticity:** Content created by real customers is more relatable.
- **Social Proof:** Seeing others use and love your products builds credibility.
- **Engagement:** Encouraging users to create content fosters community involvement.

2. Encouraging UGC

- Run contests or campaigns that incentivize participation.

- - **Example:** "Share your favorite recipe using our product and tag us to win!"
- Create branded hashtags to organize and track submissions.
- Celebrate contributors by reposting their content and giving them a shoutout.

Interactive Technologies: Fostering Deeper Connections

Interactive content enhances engagement by encouraging users to actively participate.

1. Augmented Reality (AR)

- **Why It Works:** AR experiences are immersive and memorable.
- **Examples of AR Content:**
  - Virtual try-ons for fashion or beauty products.
  - Custom Instagram or Snapchat filters featuring your brand.

2. Polls, Quizzes, and Q&A Sessions

- **Why It Works:** Interactive features spark curiosity and make your audience feel heard.
- **How to Use Them:**
  - Ask your followers to vote on their favorite product designs or flavors.

- Host live Q&A sessions to address audience questions in real time.

3. Live Sessions

- **Why It Works:** Live content feels exclusive and fosters a sense of community.
- **How to Leverage Live:**
  - Announce product launches or updates.
  - Host interviews or collaborations with influencers.

Content creation is at the core of social media marketing success. By leveraging the power of storytelling, choosing the right formats, and designing shareable content, you can engage your audience and inspire them to take action. Additionally, incorporating user-generated content and interactive technologies will deepen connections and build long-term loyalty.

Remember, content that converts isn't just about clicks or likes—it's about creating a meaningful impact that drives growth and aligns with your brand's mission. With the strategies outlined in this chapter, you're ready to craft content that captivates and converts in today's dynamic digital world.

CHAPTER 5: The Magic of Interactive and Immersive Content

As social media evolves, so does the way audiences engage with content. Gone are the days when static posts and one-sided communication were enough to captivate followers. Today, the most successful brands are those that create interactive and immersive experiences that invite participation, foster deeper connections, and leave a lasting impression.

In this chapter, we'll explore how interactive technologies like augmented reality (AR), polls, quizzes, live sessions, and AI-powered personalization can transform your social media strategy. By embracing these tools, you'll not only boost engagement but also position your brand as innovative and forward-thinking in the eyes of your audience.

Using Augmented Reality (AR) for Campaigns

Augmented reality (AR) bridges the gap between the physical and digital worlds, creating an engaging and immersive experience that captures attention and encourages interaction.

1. The Rise of AR in Social Media

- Platforms like Instagram, Snapchat, and TikTok have popularized AR filters and effects.
- AR enhances user engagement by offering a fun, interactive way to experience your brand.
    - **Example:** A makeup brand allows users to "try on" lipstick shades using AR filters.

2. How to Use AR in Campaigns

a. Branded AR Filters

- Create custom filters that incorporate your logo, products, or themes.
    - **Example:** A travel agency designs an AR filter that places users in exotic destinations.
- Encourage followers to use the filter and share their creations, boosting brand visibility.

b. AR Product Demos

- Allow users to interact with your products virtually.
    - **Example:** A furniture brand enables users to visualize how a sofa would look in their living room.

c. Gamified Experiences

- Design AR-based games that tie into your brand story.
    - **Example:** A coffee shop creates an AR scavenger hunt where users collect virtual coffee beans to win rewards.

3. Tools for Creating AR Content

- **Spark AR (Meta):** For designing AR effects on Instagram and Facebook.
- **Lens Studio (Snapchat):** For building interactive Snapchat lenses.
- **8thWall:** For advanced, web-based AR experiences.

Polls, Quizzes, and Live Sessions for Engagement

Interactive features like polls, quizzes, and live sessions are simple yet powerful tools for fostering meaningful engagement. They not only encourage participation but also provide valuable insights into your audience's preferences and interests.

1. Polls and Quizzes

a. Why They Work

- People love sharing their opinions and testing their knowledge.
- These tools make followers feel involved and valued.

b. How to Use Polls and Quizzes

- **Polls:**

- Ask fun, brand-relevant questions (e.g., "Which coffee flavor do you prefer: vanilla or hazelnut?").
- Use polls for product development by gathering audience preferences.
- **Quizzes:**
  - Create interactive quizzes that educate or entertain (e.g., "Which skincare routine suits your personality?").
  - Gamify the experience by offering discounts or rewards for participation.

c. Best Platforms for Polls and Quizzes

- Instagram Stories, Twitter polls, and interactive quizzes on websites or apps.

2. Live Sessions

a. Why Live Content Matters

- Live videos are authentic, immediate, and encourage real-time interaction.
- They create a sense of exclusivity and urgency.

b. Types of Live Sessions

- **Product Launches:** Showcase new offerings and answer audience questions.
- **Q&A Sessions:** Build trust by addressing customer inquiries directly.

- **Behind-the-Scenes:** Humanize your brand by sharing day-to-day operations or team interactions.

c. Tips for Successful Live Sessions

- Announce the live session in advance to build anticipation.
- Interact with viewers by responding to comments and questions during the session.
- Save and repurpose the live session as additional content for later use.

Creating Personalized Experiences with AI

Personalization is no longer a luxury—it's an expectation. With AI-driven tools, brands can deliver tailored experiences that make followers feel seen, understood, and valued.

1. Why Personalization Matters

- **Relevance:** Personalized content resonates more deeply with audiences.
- **Engagement:** People are more likely to engage with content that speaks to their unique preferences.
- **Loyalty:** Customers appreciate brands that take the time to understand their needs.

2. AI-Powered Personalization Strategies

a. Dynamic Content Recommendations

- Use AI to suggest relevant products, articles, or videos based on user behavior.
    - **Example:** A fitness app recommends workout routines based on the user's past activity.

b. Chatbots and Messaging

- Implement AI-driven chatbots to provide instant, personalized customer support.
    - **Example:** An online retailer's chatbot assists users with size recommendations and product availability.

c. Hyper-Targeted Ads

- Leverage AI to create ads that are tailored to specific demographics and interests.
    - **Example:** A travel brand targets ads for beach vacations to users who frequently engage with summer-related content.

d. Personalized Emails and Notifications

- Use AI tools to send customized emails with product recommendations, reminders, and exclusive offers.
    - **Example:** A streaming service sends notifications about new releases based on viewing history.

Integrating Interactive and Immersive Content into Your Strategy

To truly harness the power of interactive and immersive content, it's essential to integrate these tools strategically.

1. Combine Multiple Features

- Use AR filters to complement a live product launch.
- Pair quizzes with personalized recommendations based on results.

2. Analyze Performance

- Track engagement metrics to understand which interactive features resonate most with your audience.
- Use insights to refine your approach and continuously improve your strategy.

3. Stay Ahead of Trends

- Keep an eye on emerging technologies and platforms to ensure your strategy remains innovative and relevant.
- Experiment with new features as they become available, such as AI-generated content or virtual reality experiences.

Interactive and immersive content has transformed the social media marketing landscape, offering endless opportunities to engage audiences in meaningful ways. By leveraging AR, polls, quizzes, live sessions, and AI-driven personalization, you can create experiences that captivate, entertain, and convert.

As you embrace these tools, remember that authenticity and value should remain at the core of your strategy. Audiences crave connection, and interactive content is your gateway to building stronger, lasting relationships with them. With these insights and strategies, you're ready to bring the magic of interactive content to life and take your social media marketing to the next level.

CHAPTER 6: Harnessing User-Generated Content (UGC)

User-generated content (UGC) is one of the most powerful tools in modern social media marketing. It's authentic, cost-effective, and builds trust among audiences. When your customers, followers, or fans create content featuring your brand, they're not just amplifying your reach; they're endorsing your value.

This chapter dives deep into how to encourage and showcase UGC, foster community loyalty, and strategically leverage influencers and brand ambassadors to amplify your message. By mastering the art of UGC, you can transform your audience into active contributors and advocates for your brand, strengthening connections and driving growth.

Encouraging and Showcasing UGC

1. Why UGC Matters

- **Authenticity:** UGC feels more genuine than branded content, making it highly relatable to audiences.
- **Engagement:** People love seeing their contributions acknowledged by brands they admire.
- **Cost-Effectiveness:** Your audience creates valuable content for you, reducing production costs.

2. Strategies to Encourage UGC

a. Create Branded Hashtags

- Design a memorable and relevant hashtag for customers to tag their content.
  - **Example:** Coca-Cola's #share a coke campaign encouraged people to share photos of personalized Coke bottles.
- Regularly promote your hashtag to increase visibility.

b. Run Contests and Challenges

- Incentivize content creation by offering prizes for the best submissions.
  - **Example:** A fitness brand invites users to share their workout videos using a branded hashtag for a chance to win a free subscription.
- Challenges, such as TikTok trends, can go viral, expanding your reach organically.

c. Ask for Reviews and Testimonials

- Encourage customers to post about their experiences with your products or services.
  - **Example:** A hotel chain requests guests to share vacation photos for a chance to be featured on their social media pages.
- Offer a small incentive, such as a discount, to motivate participation.

3. Best Practices for Showcasing UGC

a. Repost and Credit

- Share user content on your platforms while giving proper credit to the creator.
    - This acknowledgment builds goodwill and encourages others to contribute.
- Platforms like Instagram and TikTok make it easy to share posts with proper attribution.

b. Create UGC Highlight Reels

- Combine multiple user submissions into engaging videos or carousel posts.
    - **Example:** A fashion brand creates a reel showcasing customers wearing their outfits during the holidays.

c. Incorporate UGC into Marketing Campaigns

- Use UGC in paid advertisements, product pages, or promotional materials to build trust.
    - **Stat:** 79% of people say UGC highly impacts their purchasing decisions.

Building Community Loyalty Through Involvement

UGC isn't just about content—it's about community. Encouraging your audience to participate fosters a sense of belonging and loyalty to your brand.

1. The Psychology of Involvement

   - People are more likely to engage with a brand they feel connected to.
   - Being featured by a brand can create excitement and deepen loyalty.

2. Strategies to Build Loyalty Through UGC

a. Celebrate Your Audience

   - Highlight top contributors with shoutouts, exclusive perks, or special recognition.
     - **Example:** A beauty brand creates a monthly "Fan of the Month" feature for its most engaged followers.

b. Host Interactive Events

   - Organize live sessions, Q&A events, or virtual meetups where audience contributions are showcased.
     - **Example:** A gaming company hosts a live stream where fan-created mods are featured and discussed.

c. Reward Participation

   - Offer loyalty points, discounts, or early access to products for users who actively create and share content.

3. Building a Culture of Participation

- Make it clear that everyone's voice matters and contributions are valued.
- Use inclusive language in your campaigns to invite participation from a diverse audience.
  - **Example:** "We'd love to see how YOU use our product—tag us for a chance to be featured!"

Leveraging Influencers and Brand Ambassadors

While UGC is typically created by everyday users, influencers and brand ambassadors can amplify its impact by introducing your brand to their engaged audiences.

1. Understanding the Role of Influencers and Ambassadors

- **Influencers:** Content creators with significant followings who can drive awareness and engagement for your brand.
- **Brand Ambassadors:** Loyal customers or fans who represent your brand long-term, often creating UGC.

2. Strategies for Partnering with Influencers

a. Identify the Right Influencers

- Look for influencers whose values align with your brand and who resonate with your target audience.

- **Example:** A sustainable fashion brand partners with eco-conscious influencers to promote its clothing line.

b. Collaborate on Content Creation

- Encourage influencers to create authentic content using your products or services.
- Allow them creative freedom while ensuring your brand message is clearly conveyed.

c. Measure Impact

- Track metrics like engagement, reach, and conversions to evaluate the success of influencer campaigns.

3. Building a Brand Ambassador Program

a. Identify Ambassadors

- Look for passionate customers or employees who already advocate for your brand.
  - **Example:** A fitness brand invites loyal users of its app to become ambassadors.

b. Provide Exclusive Perks

- Offer ambassadors free products, discounts, or early access to new releases in exchange for regular content creation.

c. Create a Supportive Community

- Foster a sense of belonging by connecting ambassadors with each other and involving them in brand decisions.

Integrating UGC into Your Broader Strategy

To maximize the impact of UGC, it's important to align it with your overall marketing strategy.

1. Combine UGC with Paid Campaigns

- Use high-quality UGC as creative assets for ads to add authenticity and credibility.

2. Monitor and Respond to UGC

- Regularly engage with user-generated content by liking, commenting, and sharing.
- Address negative or inaccurate content promptly to maintain your brand's reputation.

3. Stay Consistent

- Make UGC a recurring element of your content calendar to keep the momentum going.

Harnessing user-generated content is about more than just collecting posts—it's about building relationships, fostering loyalty, and amplifying your brand's message. Whether it's through branded hashtags, contests, influencer partnerships, or ambassador programs, UGC can transform your audience from passive consumers into active contributors and advocates.

By integrating UGC into your strategy, celebrating your community, and leveraging the power of influencers, you'll create a vibrant ecosystem of engagement and trust. With the tools and insights in this chapter, you're ready to unlock the magic of UGC and take your social media marketing to the next level.

: **PART THREE**

Platform-Specific Strategies

Social media platforms are as diverse as the audiences they serve. Each platform comes with its own set of features, audience behaviors, and unique opportunities for growth. To succeed in social media marketing, understanding these nuances is essential.

In this part, we will explore platform-specific strategies that help you tailor your approach to maximize engagement, reach, and results. Whether you're leveraging the visual appeal of Instagram, the conversational tone of Twitter, or the professional networking opportunities on LinkedIn, adapting your strategies to each platform is key to building a strong presence and achieving your goals.

This section provides actionable insights into the strengths and best practices for major platforms, helping you determine where to focus your efforts and how to craft content that resonates with the unique audiences on each. With these strategies, you'll be equipped to harness the full potential of social media's ever-expanding landscape.

Let's dive in and discover how to unlock success on the platforms that matter most to your brand.

CHAPTER 7: Dominating Facebook and Instagram

Facebook and Instagram remain two of the most powerful platforms for businesses to connect with their audiences. While each platform has unique characteristics, they are interconnected under the Meta umbrella, offering robust tools for marketing, community building, and sales. This chapter explores how to dominate these platforms by leveraging their features, understanding their audiences, and creating impactful campaigns that drive engagement and revenue.

Understanding Facebook and Instagram Features and Demographics

1. Why Facebook and Instagram Matter

- **Facebook** is ideal for community engagement, customer support, and multi-generational outreach.
- **Instagram** thrives on visual storytelling, attracting younger, trend-savvy audiences.

2. Audience Demographics

- **Facebook:**
    - Predominantly used by adults aged 25–55+.
    - Popular for family-oriented content, group discussions, and local business promotions.
- **Instagram:**

- Preferred by users aged 18–34.
- Focuses on aesthetics, trends, and short-form visual content.

3. Key Features of Both Platforms

Facebook Features:

- Groups for niche communities.
- Events for promotions and announcements.
- Ads with extensive targeting options.

Instagram Features:

- Shopping tags and product stickers.
- Stories, reels, and carousel posts for visual content.
- Creator tools for partnerships and sponsored content.

Using Facebook Groups for Community Building

1. Why Facebook Groups Are Powerful

- Groups foster a sense of exclusivity and belonging, encouraging deeper engagement.
- They allow direct communication with your audience, creating stronger brand relationships.

2. Strategies for Successful Groups

a. Define Your Group's Purpose

- Create a group aligned with your brand values and audience interests.
    - **Example:** A fitness brand forms a "Healthy Living Community" to share tips and motivation.

b. Provide Value to Members

- Share exclusive content, host live Q&A sessions, and offer early access to product launches.
    - Encourage discussions by posing questions and sharing user-generated content.

c. Moderate and Engage Actively

- Assign moderators to maintain a positive environment.
- Regularly respond to member posts and comments to foster interaction.

3. Tools for Managing Groups

- Use Facebook's group insights to track engagement metrics.
- Schedule posts with Facebook's publishing tools to maintain consistency.

Shopping Features and Ads on Instagram

1. Instagram as a Visual Marketplace

Instagram's shopping features transform the platform into a virtual storefront, allowing users to discover, browse, and purchase directly within the app.

2. Using Instagram Shopping Features

a. Set Up an Instagram Shop

- Ensure your business account is approved for shopping.
- Link your product catalog through Meta Business Suite.

b. Leverage Product Tags and Stickers

- Use product tags in posts, stories, and reels to drive traffic to your store.
  - **Example:** A fashion brand tags products in a carousel post featuring styled outfits.

c. Optimize Your Instagram Shop

- Use high-quality product images and detailed descriptions.
- Highlight trending products and limited-time offers to create urgency.

3. Instagram Ads for Sales and Awareness

a. Types of Instagram Ads

- **Photo Ads:** Ideal for single-product promotions.
- **Carousel Ads:** Showcase multiple products or tell a story.
- **Reels Ads:** Use short-form videos for dynamic and engaging content.

b. Targeting Strategies

- Use custom audiences based on website visitors or email lists.
- Experiment with lookalike audiences to reach users similar to your customers.

Trends in Visual and Short-Form Content

1. Why Visual Content Dominates

- Humans process visuals faster than text, making them more engaging.
- Short-form content like reels and stories aligns with shrinking attention spans.

2. Formats That Work Best on Instagram and Facebook

a. Instagram Reels

- Tap into trends by using popular audio clips and hashtags.
- Keep reels under 30 seconds to maximize watch time.
    - **Example:** A beauty brand creates a reel showing a product's "before and after" transformation.

b. Facebook Stories

- Use ephemeral content to share behind-the-scenes moments or quick updates.
- Add interactive elements like polls and stickers to boost engagement.

c. Carousels and Infographics

- Carousels work well for educational or multi-step content.
    - **Example:** A financial service uses a carousel to explain budgeting tips.
- Infographics make complex information digestible and shareable.

Case Studies: Success Stories from Facebook and Instagram

1. Facebook Group Success: Peloton

- Peloton's "Official Peloton Member Page" thrives with over 450,000 members.

- The group fosters a supportive community, driving customer loyalty and retention.

2. Instagram Shopping Success: Glossier

- Glossier leverages Instagram's shopping features to showcase its minimalist beauty products.
- Frequent use of product tags and visually appealing posts leads to consistent sales.

3. Short-Form Content Success: Starbucks

- Starbucks uses Instagram reels to promote seasonal drinks with trendy music and vibrant visuals.
- These reels drive significant engagement and foot traffic during promotions.

Staying Ahead of Platform-Specific Trends

1. Monitor Algorithm Updates

- Both platforms prioritize engaging content—focus on value and interaction.
- Regularly review updates on Meta's business blog to stay informed.

2. Experiment with New Features

- Adopt new tools like Instagram's broadcast channels or Facebook's collaborative posts to stay innovative.

3. Track Performance and Adapt

- Use Meta's analytics to identify high-performing content and refine your strategy.
- Experiment with A/B testing for ads and posts to find what resonates most.

Dominating Facebook and Instagram requires a deep understanding of their unique features, audiences, and trends. By leveraging Facebook Groups for community building, tapping into Instagram's shopping ecosystem, and mastering visual and short-form content, businesses can create impactful campaigns that engage audiences and drive results.

With the tools, strategies, and real-world examples shared in this chapter, you're equipped to harness the full potential of these platforms. Keep experimenting, stay adaptable, and always prioritize creating value for your audience.

CHAPTER 8: Cracking the Code of TikTok and Emerging Platforms

TikTok has revolutionized the social media landscape with its short-form, algorithm-driven videos, captivating younger audiences and brands alike. Alongside TikTok, emerging platforms like BeReal, Clubhouse, and niche networks offer untapped opportunities for marketers seeking a competitive edge. This chapter explores how to crack the code of TikTok and strategically approach new platforms to stay ahead of the curve.

Understanding TikTok and Emerging Platforms

1. Why TikTok Matters for Brands

- TikTok is the most downloaded app globally, boasting over 1 billion active users.
- Its unique algorithm prioritizes content discovery, allowing small accounts to go viral.

2. Key Features and Audience Demographics

TikTok Features:

- **For You Page (FYP):** Content discovery hub driven by user interests.

- **Hashtags and Trends:** Vital for gaining visibility and engagement.
- **Duets and Stitching:** Tools to create collaborative or reactive content.

TikTok Audience:

- Predominantly Gen Z (16–24 years old) and Millennials (25–34 years old).
- Interests include humor, authenticity, and cultural trends.

Emerging Platforms Overview:

- **BeReal:** Promotes unfiltered, real-time photos—ideal for authentic connections.
- **Clubhouse:** Audio-focused platform for thought leadership and community building.
- **Niche Platforms:** Cater to specific industries or hobbies, such as Discord for gaming or Letterboxd for film enthusiasts.

Creating Engaging, Trendy, and Authentic Videos

1. The Power of Authenticity on TikTok

- Users prefer raw, unpolished content that feels relatable and genuine.
- Brands like Chipotle and Duolingo thrive by showing humor and humanizing their presence.

2. Tips for Creating TikTok Videos

a. Hook Viewers Immediately

- Capture attention within the first 3 seconds with eye-catching visuals or intriguing questions.
    - **Example:** A skincare brand starts a video with "What's the secret to glowing skin?"

b. Embrace TikTok Trends

- Monitor trending sounds, challenges, and hashtags. Participate in ways that align with your brand's voice.
    - **Example:** A fitness brand joins a trending dance challenge but adds workout tips in the caption.

c. Use Storytelling to Build Connection

- Narratives resonate deeply—share customer stories, brand origins, or day-in-the-life videos.

d. Leverage Visual Effects and Text Overlays

- Experiment with TikTok's editing tools, transitions, and filters to make videos visually appealing.

3. Frequency and Consistency

- Post frequently (at least 4–7 times per week) to stay visible and optimize algorithm exposure.

- Maintain consistency in tone and branding across all content.

Leveraging TikTok for Brand Awareness and Conversions

1. Building Brand Awareness

a. Collaborate with Creators

- Partner with TikTok influencers who align with your brand to reach their followers authentically.
    - **Example:** A beauty brand collaborates with a makeup artist for tutorials using its products.

b. Optimize Your Profile

- Use a recognizable profile picture and bio that highlights your value proposition. Include a link to your website or products.

c. Run TikTok Ads

- Types of TikTok ads:
    - **In-Feed Ads:** Appear in users' feeds like organic content.
    - **Branded Hashtag Challenges:** Encourage user participation in creative campaigns.
    - **TopView Ads:** Capture prime placement for maximum visibility.

2. Driving Conversions

a. Add Clear Calls-to-Action (CTAs)

- End videos with CTAs, such as "Shop now," "Learn more," or "Follow for tips."

b. Use TikTok Shopping

- Leverage TikTok's in-app shopping features to create a seamless purchasing experience.
  - **Example:** A clothing brand uses product tags on TikTok Shop for direct sales.

c. Retarget with Custom Audiences

- Utilize TikTok Ads Manager to retarget users who engaged with your content or visited your website.

Keeping an Eye on New Emerging Platforms

1. Why Emerging Platforms Matter

- They offer first-mover advantages, reduced competition, and access to niche audiences.
- Early adopters often build loyal followings before platforms become oversaturated.

2. Strategies for Exploring Emerging Platforms

a. Research and Evaluate

- Assess platforms based on audience alignment, features, and growth potential.
  - **Example:** BeReal's unfiltered content approach might suit brands targeting Gen Z.

b. Experiment with Content

- Start with a test campaign or small-scale effort to understand platform dynamics.

c. Focus on Community Building

- Use Clubhouse or Discord to foster intimate discussions and deep connections with followers.

3. Balancing Efforts Across Platforms

- Avoid spreading resources too thin. Prioritize platforms with the highest ROI potential for your brand.

Case Studies: Success Stories from TikTok and Emerging Platforms

1. TikTok Success: Ocean Spray

- **Campaign:** A viral video featuring a man drinking Ocean Spray cranberry juice while skateboarding to Fleetwood Mac.
- **Impact:** Sales surged, and the company gifted the creator a truck, amplifying PR efforts.

2. BeReal Success: Outdoor Gear Brand

- **Strategy:** Posted real-time images of their team hiking while showcasing their gear.
- **Result:** Boosted authenticity and drove customer trust.

3. Clubhouse Success: Industry Expert Panel

- **Strategy:** A tech company hosted a Clubhouse discussion on emerging trends, positioning itself as a thought leader.
- **Result:** Gained industry credibility and new leads.

Staying Ahead of Trends

1. Monitor Algorithms and Updates

- TikTok's algorithm favors engaging, fresh content. Keep an eye on updates to maintain visibility.
- Follow news about emerging platforms and adapt strategies as they evolve.

2. Innovate with Features

- Experiment with TikTok's latest features, such as augmented reality (AR) filters and live shopping.
- Explore new platform-specific tools and opportunities.

3. Stay Authentic and Relatable

- Authenticity drives engagement, especially on platforms like TikTok and BeReal. Avoid overly polished content.

Cracking the code of TikTok and emerging platforms requires adaptability, creativity, and a deep understanding of platform-specific nuances. By creating engaging, trendy, and authentic content, leveraging TikTok's features for both awareness and conversions, and strategically exploring new platforms, you can position your brand as a leader in the ever-changing social media landscape.

With the strategies, examples, and insights shared in this chapter, you're ready to tap into the immense potential of TikTok and beyond. Stay innovative, experiment boldly, and always prioritize building genuine connections with your audience.

CHAPTER 9: LinkedIn and Twitter/X for Thought Leadership

LinkedIn and Twitter/X have emerged as powerful platforms for professionals, entrepreneurs, and brands to establish thought leadership and connect with their audiences. Whether you're seeking to generate B2B leads or position yourself as an industry expert, these platforms offer unique opportunities to amplify your voice and influence.

This chapter delves into how to use LinkedIn for B2B networking and lead generation, how to leverage Twitter/X for real-time engagement, and showcases case studies of success on these professional platforms.

Using LinkedIn for B2B Networking and Lead Generation

1. Why LinkedIn Is Essential for Professionals

- LinkedIn has over **930 million users**, with the majority being professionals and decision-makers.
- It's a hub for **B2B marketing**, making it ideal for networking, thought leadership, and lead generation.

2. Key Features and Audience Demographics

LinkedIn Features:

- **Company Pages:** Showcase your brand, mission, and offerings.
- **LinkedIn Ads:** Reach targeted professionals with Sponsored Content, InMail, and more.
- **LinkedIn Groups:** Build niche communities around shared interests.
- **LinkedIn Creator Mode:** Elevate your profile with tools to grow your audience.

LinkedIn Audience:

- Predominantly professionals, executives, and business owners aged 25–54.
- Key industries: IT, healthcare, finance, marketing, and education.

3. Step-by-Step Strategies for LinkedIn Success

a. Optimize Your Profile and Company Page

- Use a professional headshot and clear headline.
- Write a compelling "About" section with key achievements and goals.
- Include a detailed summary of skills and endorsements.

b. Create Value-Driven Content

- Post industry insights, how-to guides, and thought-provoking questions.
- Use LinkedIn Articles to publish long-form content and establish expertise.

c. Engage Actively

- Comment thoughtfully on others' posts to expand your reach.
- Respond to comments on your posts to foster connections.

d. Leverage LinkedIn Ads for Lead Generation

- Use Lead Gen Forms to capture potential clients' information.
- Target specific demographics based on job title, industry, or location.

Twitter/X for Real-Time Marketing and Engagement

1. Why Twitter/X Still Matters

- Twitter/X is the go-to platform for **real-time updates**, trending topics, and live engagement.
- It's an ideal space for brands to showcase **authenticity, humor, and thought leadership**.

2. Key Features and Audience Demographics

Twitter/X Features:

- **Trending Topics and Hashtags:** Join conversations in your industry.

- **Spaces:** Host live audio discussions to engage audiences.
- **Lists:** Curate feeds from specific users for focused networking.
- **Twitter Ads:** Promote tweets or run campaigns for visibility.

Twitter/X Audience:

- Active across all age groups, with a focus on users aged 18–49.
- Used by journalists, politicians, academics, and tech-savvy audiences.

3. Step-by-Step Strategies for Twitter/X Success

a. Build a Strong Presence

- Create a recognizable handle and optimize your bio with keywords.
- Pin a tweet highlighting your mission or key offering.

b. Leverage Real-Time Trends

- Monitor trending hashtags and participate when relevant.
    - **Example:** A fintech company tweets insights during #FinTechWeek.

c. Engage in Conversations

- Reply to industry leaders' tweets to build connections.

- Host Q&A sessions or polls to engage your audience.

d. Use Twitter/X for Customer Support

- Respond quickly to customer inquiries to demonstrate responsiveness.
    - **Example:** Airlines using Twitter/X for flight updates and support.

e. Amplify Thought Leadership with Spaces

- Host live audio discussions on niche topics to position yourself as an authority.

Case Studies of Success on Professional Platforms

1. LinkedIn Success Story: HubSpot

Campaign:

- HubSpot shares frequent how-to guides, industry reports, and engaging posts about marketing best practices.

Result:

- Built a massive following of professionals, driving leads and establishing itself as a thought leader in inbound marketing.

2. Twitter/X Success Story: Wendy's

Campaign:

- Wendy's uses humor and wit to engage followers and roast competitors.

Result:

- Increased brand awareness and became one of the most followed fast-food chains on Twitter/X.

Staying Ahead of Trends and Algorithms

1. Monitor Platform Updates

- LinkedIn and Twitter/X frequently update their algorithms and features. Stay informed to adapt your strategy.

2. Consistency and Authenticity

- Post consistently while maintaining a tone that aligns with your brand's values.
- Avoid overly promotional content; focus on building trust.

3. Data-Driven Adjustments

- Use LinkedIn Analytics and Twitter/X Insights to evaluate performance.
- Adjust your content strategy based on engagement metrics and audience feedback.

LinkedIn and Twitter/X are unparalleled platforms for building thought leadership, generating leads, and connecting with professionals. By leveraging LinkedIn's focus on B2B networking and Twitter/X's real-time engagement capabilities, you can establish a dominant presence in your industry.

Use the strategies, examples, and tips outlined in this chapter to maximize your impact on these platforms. With consistent effort, creativity, and a commitment to authenticity, you'll be well-positioned to lead conversations and drive meaningful results in the digital space.

PART FOUR
Advanced Strategies and Innovations

As social media continues to evolve, the strategies that once worked may no longer suffice. To stay ahead of the competition, marketers must adapt and adopt more advanced strategies and innovations. In this section, we'll explore cutting-edge techniques that go beyond the basics and allow businesses to remain at the forefront of social media marketing. From artificial intelligence (AI) tools and augmented reality (AR) integrations to data-driven decision-making and personalization, these strategies will empower your brand to thrive in the dynamic world of digital marketing.

In this part of the book, we'll break down innovative approaches and the future of social media marketing to ensure that your business doesn't just keep up with trends but also leads the charge. Whether you are using AI for personalization, exploring the potential of AR, or mastering the latest analytics tools, this section will provide the tools and knowledge needed to elevate your social media presence to the next level. By incorporating these advanced strategies and innovations into your marketing campaigns, you'll not only capture the attention of your audience but also build lasting, meaningful connections that drive long-term success. Let's dive into the cutting-edge strategies that will define the future of social media marketing.

CHAPTER 10: The Role of AI in Social Media Marketing

Artificial Intelligence (AI) is revolutionizing social media marketing, providing unprecedented tools for content creation, audience engagement, and campaign optimization. With the ability to process massive amounts of data, predict trends, and personalize user experiences, AI is no longer a futuristic concept but a present necessity. This chapter explores how marketers can leverage AI-driven tools, predictive analytics, and chatbots to create high-impact campaigns and stay ahead of the competition.

AI-Driven Content Creation Tools

1. The Power of AI in Content Creation

AI-powered tools can analyze audience preferences and generate highly relevant, engaging content. By automating repetitive tasks, marketers can focus on strategic planning and creative execution.

2. Popular AI Tools for Social Media Content

a. Copywriting and Caption Generators

- **Tools:** ChatGPT, Jasper, Writesonic.
- **Use Case:** Generate engaging captions, blog excerpts, or ad copy tailored to your target audience.

b. Visual Content Creation Tools

- **Tools:** Canva with Magic Design, DALL-E, and Adobe Firefly.
- **Use Case:** Create professional-quality graphics, infographics, and videos in minutes.

c. Video Editing and Enhancement Tools

- **Tools:** Pictory, Lumen5, and Synthesia.
- **Use Case:** Automate video creation and subtitles, and create AI-generated avatars for explainer videos.

3. Benefits of AI-Driven Content Tools

- Faster production of high-quality content.
- Tailored outputs based on analytics and audience insights.
- Enhanced creativity through AI-powered suggestions.

Predictive Analytics for Campaign Planning

1. What Is Predictive Analytics?

Predictive analytics uses data, algorithms, and machine learning to forecast future outcomes. For social media, it helps anticipate trends, optimize campaigns, and make data-driven decisions.

2. How Predictive Analytics Enhanced Campaigns

a. Audience Insights

- Analyze audience behavior to predict engagement patterns.
- Identify the best times to post and the type of content that resonates.

b. Campaign Optimization

- Forecast the success of ad campaigns by analyzing historical performance data.
- Allocate budgets to maximize ROI based on predicted outcomes.

c. Content Trends

- Use tools like Google Trends and AI dashboards to predict trending topics.
- Stay ahead by creating content around anticipated audience interests.

3. Tools for Predictive Analytics

- **Hootsuite Insights:** For tracking trends and audience behavior.
- **Sprinklr AI:** To predict campaign performance and optimize strategy.
- **Salesforce Einstein:** For advanced AI-driven audience segmentation and prediction.

Chatbots for Instant Engagement

1. Why Chatbots Are Essential

Modern consumers expect instant responses. Chatbots provide 24/7 engagement, ensuring no query goes unanswered. They enhance customer service, streamline interactions, and improve user satisfaction.

2. Types of Chatbots for Social Media

a. Rule-Based Chatbots

- Follow pre-set rules to answer common queries.
- Ideal for FAQs and basic customer service.

b. AI-Powered Chatbots

- Use natural language processing (NLP) to understand context and provide human-like responses.
- Continuously learn and improve based on user interactions.

3. Platforms and Tools for Chatbots

- **Facebook Messenger Bots:** For automated replies and lead generation.
- **ManyChat:** Integrates with multiple platforms for advanced chatbot management.
- **ChatGPT API:** To create highly personalized and intelligent conversational bots.

4. Examples of Effective Chatbot Use

a. Lead Qualification

- Bots can ask qualifying questions to identify high-quality leads and route them to sales teams.

b. Personalized Recommendations

- Bots analyze user preferences to suggest products or services.

c. Real-Time Customer Support

- Handle inquiries such as shipping updates, refund requests, and more.

Integrating AI, AR, and Blockchain for Future Success

1. Leveraging Augmented Reality (AR)

a. What Is AR?

AR overlays digital elements onto the real world via smartphones or wearable devices.

b. Use Cases in Social Media Marketing:

- Virtual try-ons for fashion, makeup, and accessories.
- AR filters for interactive and shareable experiences (e.g., Snapchat, Instagram).

c. Examples of AR in Action:

- IKEA's AR app for furniture placement.
- Sephora's virtual makeup try-on tool.

2. Blockchain and Social Media Marketing

a. Enhancing Transparency and Trust:

- Use blockchain to verify influencer partnerships and campaign authenticity.

b. Rewarding Engagement:

- Platforms can reward users with crypto tokens for participating in campaigns.

Tips for Staying Ahead of Competitors

1. Stay Updated on AI Advancements

Follow AI research and updates to understand how tools are evolving and how they can be integrated into your strategy.

2. Experiment and Test

Continuously experiment with new AI tools, predictive analytics, and chatbots to identify what works best for your brand.

3. Invest in Training and Tools

Equip your team with the skills and resources to harness advanced technologies effectively.

AI, predictive analytics, and automation are reshaping the way brands interact with their audiences on social media. These tools not only streamline processes but also provide deeper insights and opportunities for personalization. By embracing these advanced strategies, marketers can create more engaging campaigns, foster deeper connections with their audiences, and achieve exceptional results.

Integrating innovations like AR, blockchain, and intelligent chatbots will position your brand at the cutting edge of social media marketing. With a proactive and forward-thinking approach, you'll not only adapt to the future of digital marketing—you'll help shape it.

CHAPTER 11: Paid Advertising Mastery

Paid advertising has become an essential element in any social media marketing strategy. Its potential to reach hyper-targeted audiences and drive measurable results has made it the go-to tool for businesses aiming to amplify their reach, boost engagement, and maximize ROI. However, the digital advertising landscape is evolving rapidly. Marketers must not only master the basics but also integrate advanced tools like AI, predictive analytics, and automation to stay ahead of the competition.

This chapter dives into advanced targeting strategies, high-converting ad campaign creation, and the use of performance metrics to measure and optimize success. You'll also discover how innovative technologies such as AR, blockchain, and chatbots can revolutionize your advertising approach.

Advanced Targeting Strategies

The Power of Targeting in Paid Advertising

Paid advertising's strength lies in its ability to deliver the right message to the right audience at the right time. Advanced targeting strategies enable marketers to:

- Minimize wasted ad spend.
- Increase campaign efficiency.

- Drive higher conversion rates by reaching users with genuine intent.

Key Targeting Techniques

1. Demographic Targeting

Reach audiences based on age, gender, income, location, and other demographic factors.

- **Example:** A high-end jewelry brand targeting women aged 25-45 in metropolitan areas.

2. Interest-Based Targeting

Target users who engage with specific topics or hobbies.

- **Example:** Advertising a fitness app to individuals who follow gym and workout-related pages.

3. Behavioral Targeting

Focus on actions such as recent purchases, website visits, or app usage.

- **Example:** Retargeting users who viewed a product but didn't make a purchase.

4. Lookalike Audiences

Leverage data from existing customers to find people with similar characteristics.

- Platforms like Facebook, LinkedIn, and Google Ads provide robust lookalike audience tools.

5. Contextual Targeting

Place ads on websites or content relevant to your product or service.

- **Example:** Displaying a cooking gadget ad on recipe blogs.

Creating High-Converting Ad Campaigns

Essential Components of Effective Ads

1. Captivating Headlines and Copy

- Keep headlines short, clear, and attention-grabbing.
- Use compelling copy to emphasize value propositions and pain points.
- **Example:** "Boost Your Productivity with Our AI-Driven Planner!"

2. Engaging Visuals

Visual elements play a crucial role in capturing user attention.

- High-quality images or videos aligned with your brand voice.
- Use bright colors and clear, focused designs.

3. Strong Call-to-Actions (CTAs)

- Use action-oriented phrases that prompt immediate responses.
- **Examples:** "Shop Now," "Learn More," or "Try It Free."

Formats That Drive Results

1. Video Ads

Videos outperform static images in engagement, particularly on platforms like Instagram and TikTok.

- Tips: Use captions for silent viewers and keep videos under 60 seconds.

2. Carousel Ads

Perfect for showcasing multiple products, features, or services in one ad.

3. Interactive Ads

Include polls, quizzes, or AR filters to encourage participation and engagement.

Measuring Success with Performance Metrics

Why Metrics Matter

Metrics provide insights into what's working and what needs adjustment. Without proper tracking, even the best campaigns can fall short.

Key Metrics to Monitor

1. Click-Through Rate (CTR)

Measures how many people clicked your ad compared to how many saw it.

2. Conversion Rate (CVR)

Tracks the percentage of users who completed a desired action after clicking the ad.

3. Return on Ad Spend (ROAS)

Calculates the revenue generated for every dollar spent on advertising.

4. Impressions and Reach

Understand how many people saw your ad and how many times.

5. Cost Per Acquisition (CPA)

Measures how much you're spending to acquire a customer.

Tools for Tracking and Analysis

- **Google Analytics:** Detailed insights into ad performance and user behavior.
- **Facebook Ads Manager:** Tracks performance across multiple campaigns.
- **Hootsuite Ads:** Simplifies ROI tracking across various platforms.

Leveraging Innovative Technologies in Paid Advertising

AI-Driven Campaign Optimization

AI tools can automate targeting, bidding, and ad creative adjustments in real-time.

- **Examples:** Google Ads' Smart Bidding or Facebook's Dynamic Creative Optimization.

Augmented Reality (AR) in Ads

AR ads allow users to interact with products virtually.

- **Example:** A furniture retailer enabling users to see how a sofa fits in their living room.
- Platforms: Instagram and Snapchat are leading in AR ad formats.

Chatbots for Instant Engagement

Integrate chatbots with your paid campaigns to provide instant responses to inquiries.

- **Example:** A chatbot initiating conversations with users who click on your Facebook ad.

Blockchain for Ad Transparency

Blockchain can verify ad impressions and ensure transparency in ad spending.

- This reduces fraud and builds trust with advertisers.

Tips for Optimizing Paid Advertising ROI

1. **Test and Iterate**: Run A/B tests for headlines, visuals, and CTAs.
2. **Monitor Trends**: Stay updated on algorithm changes and user behavior shifts.
3. **Budget Wisely**: Allocate more budget to high-performing campaigns.
4. **Leverage Retargeting**: Follow up with users who interacted with your brand but didn't convert.

Mastering paid advertising requires a combination of strategic targeting, creative execution, and a data-driven mindset. By embracing advanced technologies such as AI and AR, focusing on clear metrics, and staying agile, businesses can turn social media ads into powerful revenue drivers. This chapter equips you with the tools and insights to create campaigns that not only reach but also resonate with your audience, ensuring long-term success in the competitive digital landscape.

CHAPTER 12: Leveraging Influencer Partnerships

Influencer marketing has emerged as a cornerstone of modern social media strategies. Influencers—content creators with dedicated followings—have the power to shape opinions, drive trends, and inspire action. Partnering with the right influencers can amplify brand visibility, foster trust, and deliver exceptional ROI when executed strategically.

This chapter explores how to identify the perfect influencers for your brand, build sustainable partnerships, and measure the success of influencer campaigns. By integrating innovative tools like AI and predictive analytics into your influencer strategy, you'll unlock new opportunities to stay ahead in the competitive digital landscape.

Finding the Right Influencers for Your Brand

Why Influencer Partnerships Work

Influencers bring authenticity and credibility to brand messaging. Unlike traditional advertising, their endorsements feel personal, making them more likely to resonate with audiences.

Types of Influencers

- **Mega-Influencers:** Celebrities or public figures with millions of followers.
  - Pros: Massive reach.
  - Cons: High cost, less niche engagement.
- **Macro-Influencers:** Established creators with 100K–1M followers.
  - Pros: Good reach and moderate engagement.
  - Cons: Still relatively expensive.
- **Micro-Influencers:** Creators with 10K–100K followers in a specific niche.
  - Pros: High engagement, niche relevance, cost-effective.
  - Cons: Limited reach.
- **Nano-Influencers:** Everyday people with 1K–10K followers and strong local or niche influence.
  - Pros: Authenticity and strong personal connections.
  - Cons: Very limited reach.

Steps to Identify the Right Influencers

1. Define Your Goals

Clarify what you aim to achieve with influencer partnerships:

- Boost brand awareness.
- Drive website traffic.
- Increase conversions.
- Build community loyalty.

2. Know Your Audience

Understand your target audience's demographics, interests, and behaviors. Choose influencers whose followers align with these profiles.

3. Assess Authenticity and Engagement

Look beyond follower count:

- Check the quality of interactions (comments, shares, likes).
- Beware of fake followers or engagement pods.

4. Use AI and Analytics Tools

Advanced platforms like **AspireIQ**, **Upfluence**, and **Traackr** can help you analyze influencer data and match you with ideal candidates.

Building Long-Term Relationships

Why Long-Term Relationships Matter

Sustainable partnerships yield better results than one-off collaborations. A consistent association with influencers strengthens brand credibility and fosters loyalty among their followers.

Strategies for Building Meaningful Connections

1. Start with Authentic Outreach

Avoid generic pitches. Personalize your approach to highlight why their content aligns with your brand values.

2. Offer Mutual Value

Partnerships should be a two-way street. Provide influencers with:

- Fair compensation.
- Creative freedom.
- Access to exclusive products or events.

3. Involve Influencers in Campaign Planning

Collaborate with influencers on:

- Messaging that resonates with their audience.
- Content formats and themes.
- Scheduling and posting strategies.

4. Support Their Growth

Help influencers build their brand by:

- Sharing their content on your channels.
- Offering insights or tools to enhance their creative process.

5. Nurture Relationships Beyond Campaigns

Stay engaged even when not actively collaborating. Congratulate them on milestones or share their unrelated content to maintain goodwill.

Measuring the ROI of Influencer Campaigns

Why ROI Matters

Every partnership should deliver measurable results. Calculating ROI ensures your investment aligns with business objectives and informs future strategies.

Key Metrics to Track

1. Engagement Metrics

- Likes, comments, shares, and clicks.
- Measure the quality of interactions, not just the quantity.

2. Reach and Impressions

- How many people saw the influencer's content?
- Were these impressions relevant to your target audience?

3. Conversion Metrics

- Sales generated via affiliate links or discount codes.
- Website traffic and form submissions.

4. Audience Growth

- New followers on your social media platforms.
- Increased email subscribers or app downloads.

5. Brand Sentiment

- Analyze comments or direct feedback to gauge audience perception.

Tools for ROI Analysis

- **Google Analytics:** Tracks website traffic and conversions.
- **Bitly or UTM Codes:** Monitors clicks on links shared by influencers.
- **Influencer-Specific Dashboards:** Many platforms like Instagram now offer detailed insights for brand collaborations.

Integrating Innovation into Influencer Partnerships

AI-Powered Collaboration Tools

AI simplifies the influencer marketing process by:

- Automating influencer discovery and outreach.
- Providing data-driven recommendations for campaign optimization.

Example: AI tools can analyze past influencer campaigns to predict which type of content will perform best.

Leveraging AR and Interactive Content

Collaborate with influencers to create augmented reality filters or gamified experiences.

- **Example:** Beauty brands partnering with influencers to promote AR makeup trials on Instagram.

Blockchain for Transparency

Blockchain technology can validate influencer metrics and ensure transparency in compensation and deliverables.

- **Example:** Smart contracts outlining campaign terms on a blockchain platform.

Tips for Scaling Influencer Campaigns

1. **Diversify Your Influencer Portfolio**
   Work with a mix of micro, macro, and nano-influencers to balance reach and engagement.

2. **Test and Learn**
   Start small, analyze results, and scale partnerships that deliver the best ROI.
3. **Repurpose Content**
   Use influencer-generated content across your own channels to maximize value.
4. **Stay Ahead of Trends**
   Monitor new platforms and emerging influencer niches to identify fresh opportunities.

Influencer partnerships are more than just a trend—they are a powerful tool for building authentic connections and driving tangible results. By choosing the right influencers, fostering long-term relationships, and leveraging advanced technologies like AI and blockchain, businesses can unlock the full potential of influencer marketing. Whether your goal is to increase brand awareness or drive sales, the strategies in this chapter provide a roadmap to success in the dynamic world of social media marketing.

PART FIVE

Measuring Success and Continuous Improvement

In the rapidly evolving landscape of social media marketing, the key to staying competitive lies in ongoing evaluation and adaptation. Without accurate measurement and a commitment to continuous improvement, even the most creative strategies can fall short of their potential.

This section focuses on helping readers understand the importance of tracking performance, analyzing results, and leveraging insights to refine their social media marketing efforts. It equips marketers with the tools and techniques to assess the effectiveness of their campaigns, pinpoint areas for improvement, and implement data-driven strategies that yield long-term success.

The Importance of Measuring Success

Measuring success in social media marketing goes beyond vanity metrics like likes and follows. True success lies in understanding how your efforts contribute to overarching business objectives, whether that's increasing brand awareness, generating leads, or driving sales.

Performance measurement allows you to:

- **Identify what works:** Highlight high-performing campaigns and replicate their success.
- **Optimize underperforming areas:** Address gaps in strategy and execution.
- **Align efforts with goals:** Ensure every activity contributes to your broader objectives.

Why Continuous Improvement Matters

The digital space is constantly changing. Algorithms evolve, consumer preferences shift, and new technologies emerge. To thrive in this dynamic environment, marketers must adopt a mindset of continuous learning and experimentation.

By embracing a culture of improvement, you can:

- Stay ahead of competitors by adopting new trends and tools.
- Build stronger connections with your audience through relevant, timely content.
- Maximize ROI by refining your approach based on real-world data.

What to Expect in This Part

This part of the book delves into actionable strategies and frameworks for measuring and improving social media performance. You'll learn how to:

- **Track the right metrics:** Distinguish between vanity metrics and actionable KPIs.
- **Conduct effective audits:** Regularly assess the health of your social media presence.
- **Use analytics tools:** Leverage platforms like Google Analytics, native social media insights, and third-party tools to collect and interpret data.

- **Experiment and adapt:** Test new ideas and optimize based on outcomes.

With the guidance in this section, you'll develop a data-driven approach to social media marketing, enabling you to make informed decisions and continually elevate your campaigns. Whether you're an entrepreneur, marketer, or social media professional, mastering the art of measurement and improvement will position you for sustained success in the digital age.

CHAPTER 13: Data-Driven Decision Making

In today's fast-paced digital world, data is the backbone of effective social media marketing. While creativity and innovation are crucial, it's the ability to measure, analyze, and act on data that separates successful marketers from the rest. Data-driven decision-making empowers businesses to optimize their campaigns, stay ahead of trends, and achieve measurable results.

This chapter explores essential analytics tools, how to interpret data effectively, and actionable strategies for refining your social media efforts. By mastering these techniques, you'll be equipped to make informed decisions that drive meaningful engagement and business growth.

Essential Social Media Analytics Tools

Why Analytics Tools Matter

Analytics tools provide the insights needed to understand what's working, what's not, and where to focus your efforts. They offer data on audience behavior, content performance, and overall campaign success, enabling marketers to make informed adjustments.

Top Analytics Tools to Leverage

1. Native Social Media Insights

    - **Facebook Insights**: Tracks page views, post engagement, and audience demographics.
    - **Instagram Insights**: Provides data on follower growth, reach, and content interactions.
    - **LinkedIn Analytics**: Ideal for tracking B2B engagement, including post views and audience demographics.
    - **TikTok Analytics**: Focuses on video performance, audience growth, and trending content.

2. Comprehensive Platforms

    - **Google Analytics**: Tracks website traffic driven by social media campaigns and measures conversion rates.
    - **Hootsuite Analytics**: Offers multi-platform tracking for engagement, clicks, and ROI.
    - **Sprout Social**: Provides advanced reporting and tools for sentiment analysis.

3. Specialized Tools

    - **BuzzSumo**: Monitors content trends and competitor performance.
    - **Brandwatch**: Tracks brand mentions and sentiment across platforms.
    - **Tableau**: Visualizes complex data for deeper insights.

Key Features to Look For in Analytics Tools

- User-friendly dashboards.
- Cross-platform integration.
- Real-time data tracking.
- Customizable reporting features.

How to Interpret and Act on Insights

Understanding Key Performance Metrics (KPIs)

Focusing on the right metrics is essential for actionable insights.

Engagement Metrics

- **Likes, Comments, and Shares**: Indicators of audience interaction and content relevance.
- **Click-Through Rates (CTR)**: Measures how effectively content drives traffic to your website.
- **Follower Growth**: Tracks the expansion of your audience over time.

Reach and Impressions

- **Reach**: The number of unique users who see your content.
- **Impressions**: The total number of times your content is displayed.

Conversion Metrics

- **Leads Generated**: How many users take actions like signing up or downloading content.
- **Sales or Revenue**: The direct business impact of social media efforts.

Steps to Interpret Data Effectively

1. **Compare Metrics to Goals**: Align analytics with predefined objectives (e.g., increasing engagement or boosting sales).
2. **Identify Patterns**: Look for recurring trends in high-performing posts or campaigns.
3. **Segment Your Data**: Break down analytics by audience demographics, post types, or platforms.

Turning Insights into Action

- Use data to identify top-performing content and replicate its elements (format, tone, timing).
- Target underperforming areas with A/B testing to identify improvements.
- Adjust your content calendar based on audience activity peaks.

Tracking Trends Over Time

Why Long-Term Tracking is Crucial

Trends offer valuable insights into audience behavior, platform changes, and emerging opportunities. By monitoring these shifts, you can adapt your strategy proactively.

Steps for Effective Trend Tracking

1. Monitor Platform Updates

Social media platforms frequently update algorithms, introduce new features, or shift content priorities. Staying informed ensures you remain competitive.

2. Analyze Competitor Performance

Use tools like BuzzSumo or SEMrush to observe competitor campaigns and learn from their successes and failures.

3. Leverage Predictive Analytics

Advanced tools like Sprinklr or Salesforce Einstein can forecast trends based on historical data, helping you plan for the future.

Applying Trend Data to Strategy

- Experiment with emerging content formats (e.g., Instagram Reels or TikTok trends).
- Invest in platforms where your target audience is growing.
- Test new ad types or targeting features as they become available.

The Importance of A/B Testing

What is A/B Testing?

A/B testing involves creating two versions of content or campaigns to determine which performs better. For example, testing different captions, visuals, or CTAs can provide insights into audience preferences.

How to Run Effective A/B Tests

1. **Define a Clear Objective**: What are you testing for? (e.g., higher engagement, better CTR).
2. **Change One Variable at a Time**: This ensures the results are tied to a specific change.
3. **Track Results Over Time**: Collect sufficient data before making conclusions.

Examples of A/B Testing

- **Ad Campaigns**: Test different headlines or target audiences.
- **Content Formats**: Compare performance of videos vs. images.
- **Posting Times**: Experiment with different days or hours.

Practical Tools for Tracking and Refinement

Social Listening Tools

- **Mention**: Monitors online conversations about your brand.
- **Brandwatch**: Tracks sentiment and emerging topics in your industry.

Optimization Platforms

- **CoSchedule**: Helps refine content calendars based on past performance.
- **HubSpot**: Combines CRM and social analytics for streamlined optimization.

Dashboards for Consolidated Insights

- Use tools like Tableau or Power BI to centralize data from multiple platforms and visualize trends.

Data-driven decision-making is the foundation of successful social media marketing. By leveraging advanced analytics tools, interpreting key metrics, and embracing strategies like A/B testing, businesses can optimize their efforts for maximum impact. Tracking trends over time ensures you remain agile in a constantly evolving digital landscape.

The strategies outlined in this chapter empower marketers to not only measure their success but also refine their approach for continuous growth. With the right mindset and tools, you can transform data into actionable insights and unlock the full potential of your social media campaigns.

CHAPTER 14: A/B Testing and Optimization

In the competitive and ever-evolving world of social media marketing, continuous improvement is the key to long-term success. A/B testing, also known as split testing, is a powerful strategy that allows marketers to refine their campaigns based on real-world results. By experimenting with different variables, implementing data-driven changes, and staying agile in response to emerging trends, businesses can maximize their social media ROI.

This chapter dives into the principles of A/B testing, the process of optimization, and actionable strategies to ensure your marketing efforts remain effective and adaptable in a rapidly changing digital environment.

Testing Content, Ads, and Campaigns

What is A/B Testing?

A/B testing involves creating two versions of a single element—such as a post, ad, or landing page—and comparing their performance to determine which one resonates better with your audience. By isolating variables, you can identify what drives engagement, clicks, and conversions.

Elements to Test in Social Media Marketing

1. Content Variables

- **Headlines or Captions**: Compare different tones, lengths, or CTAs.
- **Visuals**: Test images versus videos, or different styles of graphics.
- **Post Timing**: Analyze performance across different days and times.

2. Ad Campaign Variables

- **Target Audiences**: Experiment with demographics, interests, or behaviors.
- **Formats**: Compare carousel ads with single-image ads.
- **Budget Allocation**: Test performance with varying spend levels.

3. Campaign Strategies

- **Landing Pages**: Measure how different designs or CTAs impact conversions.
- **Promotional Offers**: Test discounts, free trials, or limited-time offers.

How to Run Effective A/B Tests

1. **Define a Clear Goal**: Identify the metric you aim to improve (e.g., engagement, CTR, conversions).

2. **Test One Variable at a Time**: Changing multiple elements simultaneously can skew results.
3. **Ensure Sufficient Sample Size**: Collect enough data to make statistically significant conclusions.
4. **Analyze Results Objectively**: Use analytics tools to evaluate which version performs better.

Implementing Changes Based on Results

Interpreting A/B Test Outcomes

Key Metrics to Monitor

- **Engagement Rate**: Indicates audience interest and interaction.
- **Click-Through Rate (CTR)**: Shows how effectively your content drives traffic.
- **Conversion Rate**: Measures how well your campaign achieves its intended goal.

Common Scenarios and Actions

- **If Visual Content Performs Better**: Shift focus to high-quality images or videos.
- **If Engagement Drops on Certain Days**: Adjust your posting schedule.
- **If One Audience Segment Converts Better**: Redirect more budget toward that segment.

Making Data-Driven Adjustments

1. **Optimize Underperforming Elements**: Use insights to refine captions, visuals, or targeting.
2. **Scale Successful Strategies**: Double down on high-performing campaigns or formats.
3. **Test Again**: Social media trends change quickly; re-test to ensure continued effectiveness.

Staying Agile in a Rapidly Changing Environment

The Need for Flexibility

Social media platforms frequently update algorithms, introduce new features, and evolve user behavior. Staying agile ensures that your strategies remain relevant and effective.

Building an Agile Social Media Strategy

1. Monitor Industry Trends

Stay informed about changes in platform algorithms, emerging formats (e.g., reels, stories), and audience preferences. Tools like Google Trends and BuzzSumo can help.

2. Adopt a Growth Mindset

View underperforming campaigns as opportunities to learn and improve. Experimentation is vital for growth.

3. Embrace Real-Time Optimization

- Use live analytics dashboards to monitor campaign performance as it happens.
- Be prepared to adjust targeting, budgets, or creative assets on the fly.

Practical Examples and Tools for Optimization

Real-World Examples

1. A/B Testing in Ads

A clothing brand ran two Facebook ads: one showcasing a lifestyle image and another highlighting product features. The lifestyle ad received 40% higher engagement, prompting the brand to prioritize similar visuals in future campaigns.

2. Post Timing Experimentation

A fitness influencer tested morning versus evening posting on Instagram. Data showed higher engagement in the evening, leading to a revised content schedule.

3. Refining Landing Pages

An e-commerce site tested two versions of a landing page: one with a long-form description and another with a concise overview. The concise version converted 25% more visitors, guiding future design choices.

Essential Tools for A/B Testing and Optimization

1. Social Media Platforms

- **Facebook Ads Manager**: Built-in A/B testing for ads.
- **Instagram Insights**: Data on post performance and audience activity.
- **TikTok Analytics**: Focused on video trends and engagement metrics.

2. Third-Party Tools

- **Optimizely**: For running A/B tests across websites and apps.
- **Crazy Egg**: Provides heatmaps and click-tracking for optimization.
- **Unbounce**: Specialized in landing page testing and optimization.

The Importance of Continuous Improvement

Why Continuous Improvement Matters

Social media is not a set-it-and-forget-it channel. Regularly analyzing performance and making data-driven adjustments are critical for staying competitive.

Steps for Sustained Success

1. **Schedule Regular Reviews**: Analyze campaign performance weekly or monthly.
2. **Document Learnings**: Keep a record of what works and what doesn't for future reference.
3. **Stay Innovative**: Experiment with emerging trends, tools, and formats to remain ahead.

A/B testing and continuous optimization are vital components of a successful social media marketing strategy. By systematically testing variables, implementing changes based on insights, and staying agile in response to trends, businesses can ensure their efforts yield maximum impact.

Embrace the mindset of experimentation and improvement. Social media's dynamic nature requires marketers to be both creative and analytical, ready to pivot strategies when necessary. With the right tools, techniques, and a commitment to data-driven decisions, you can unlock your brain's full potential and achieve sustained success in the digital landscape.

PART SIX

Preparing for the Future

As we wrap up this comprehensive guide on social media marketing, it's essential to look ahead and prepare for the future. The digital marketing landscape is always evolving, with new platforms, technologies, and consumer behaviors emerging regularly. To stay competitive, businesses must not only react to these changes but also proactively adapt and innovate their strategies.

In this section, we'll explore the upcoming trends, technologies, and strategies that are likely to shape the future of social media marketing. Understanding these shifts will help you future-proof your marketing efforts and ensure that your brand continues to thrive in an ever-changing digital world.

The Impact of Emerging Technologies

The rise of artificial intelligence (AI), augmented reality (AR), blockchain, and other cutting-edge technologies is revolutionizing how businesses approach social media marketing. These technologies are transforming everything from content creation to customer engagement. As marketers, embracing these innovations early will give you a competitive edge.

1. **AI and Machine Learning:** Predictive analytics, personalized content, and automated customer service are just a few areas where AI will continue to enhance social media marketing. AI is already helping businesses create more targeted ads, improve content recommendations, and analyze user behavior to

optimize campaigns. As these technologies evolve, their potential will expand, providing even more opportunities for marketers to automate processes and deliver highly personalized experiences at scale.
2. **Augmented Reality (AR):** Social media platforms like Instagram, Snapchat, and Facebook are incorporating AR filters and immersive shopping experiences. In the coming years, AR is expected to play an even larger role in how brands engage with consumers, offering virtual try-ons, interactive product demos, and real-time product customizations.
3. **Blockchain:** While still in its early stages, blockchain technology is beginning to disrupt areas such as social media verification, digital rights management, and influencer marketing. Blockchain has the potential to offer greater transparency in ad spending and eliminate fraud, ensuring that marketers get the most value from their campaigns.

Preparing for Changing Consumer Behaviors

Consumer behavior is always in flux, and understanding how trends such as increased privacy concerns, the shift toward value-driven purchasing, and the demand for instant gratification will impact social media marketing is critical for staying ahead.

1. **Privacy and Data Protection:** With increased awareness around data privacy (think GDPR and similar regulations), consumers are more cautious about how their data is collected and used. Marketers

will need to be transparent and ethical in their data collection and use, ensuring compliance with regulations while building trust with their audience.
2. **Social Commerce and Seamless Shopping:** Social commerce is expected to grow significantly, as more consumers are buying products directly through social platforms. The lines between social networking and e-commerce are blurring, and marketers will need to optimize their strategies for seamless shopping experiences across platforms.
3. **Gen Z and Beyond:** As younger generations become the dominant force in consumer spending, businesses must adapt to their unique preferences and behaviors. These audiences value authenticity, inclusivity, and social impact, and they're more likely to engage with brands that reflect their values. Marketers will need to prioritize personalization, creativity, and transparency to capture the attention of Gen Z and future generations.

Sustainability and Ethical Marketing

The demand for brands to take a stance on social and environmental issues is growing. Consumers are becoming increasingly mindful of the ethical practices behind the products they purchase, and they want to support companies that align with their values.

Incorporating sustainability and ethical marketing practices into your strategy will not only enhance your brand image but also build a loyal, purpose-driven community. Whether through reducing environmental impact, supporting charitable causes, or advocating for social justice, businesses that demonstrate their commitment to creating a better world will stand out in a crowded marketplace.

The Importance of Adaptability and Agility

Social media marketing is a fast-paced field, and what works today might not work tomorrow. In this dynamic environment, businesses must be flexible and able to pivot quickly in response to new trends, audience shifts, or unforeseen challenges. This requires a mindset of continuous learning and improvement, staying informed about new technologies and emerging platforms, and being willing to experiment with new strategies.

As we look to the future of social media marketing, businesses that stay innovative, adapt to technological advancements, and understand shifting consumer expectations will be the ones that thrive. Some final key takeaways include:

1. **Embrace Innovation:** Stay at the forefront of emerging technologies such as AI, AR, and blockchain to differentiate your brand and improve customer experiences.

2. **Stay Consumer-Centric:** Adapt to changing consumer preferences by offering personalized, authentic, and value-driven experiences.
3. **Prioritize Agility:** Maintain flexibility in your marketing approach to quickly respond to industry shifts and new opportunities.
4. **Champion Ethical Practices:** As consumers increasingly prioritize ethical considerations, make sustainability and social responsibility integral parts of your brand's mission.

CHAPTER 15: Emerging Trends in Social Media Marketing

The social media landscape is constantly evolving, driven by new technologies, changing consumer behaviors, and the rise of innovative platforms. Staying ahead of these trends is essential for marketers who want to maintain a competitive edge and adapt to the disruptions of tomorrow. In this chapter, we'll explore two transformative trends—decentralized social media and the growing role of augmented reality (AR) and virtual reality (VR) in social media. We'll also provide actionable strategies to help marketers navigate these shifts effectively.

The Rise of Decentralized Social Media

What Is Decentralized Social Media?

Decentralized social media platforms operate on blockchain technology rather than centralized servers. Unlike traditional platforms such as Facebook or Instagram, which are controlled by corporations, decentralized platforms empower users by giving them control over their data and content. These platforms eliminate the middleman, allowing for greater transparency, privacy, and freedom of expression.

Examples of decentralized platforms include Mastodon, Minds, and Lens Protocol. While still in their infancy, these platforms are gaining traction among users who prioritize privacy and data ownership.

Why It Matters for Marketers

The shift toward decentralized social media reflects growing concerns about data privacy, censorship, and the monopolistic nature of traditional platforms. For marketers, this trend presents both challenges and opportunities:

- **Data Ownership:** Users on decentralized platforms have greater control over their data, which may limit marketers' ability to collect detailed analytics. However, it also builds trust between users and brands.
- **Niche Communities:** Decentralized platforms often attract niche audiences with specific interests, making them ideal for targeted marketing campaigns.
- **Transparency and Authenticity:** Brands must adopt more transparent and authentic strategies to thrive in decentralized ecosystems.

Strategies for Marketers

1. **Adopt Ethical Marketing Practices:** Respect user privacy and focus on building trust through transparent communication and value-driven content.
2. **Leverage Community Engagement:** Engage with niche communities authentically by participating in discussions, sharing valuable insights, and aligning with their values.

3. **Stay Agile:** Monitor emerging decentralized platforms and experiment with pilot campaigns to understand their dynamics and potential.

The Future of AR/VR in Social Media

The Rise of AR/VR in Social Media

Augmented reality (AR) and virtual reality (VR) are no longer futuristic concepts—they are transforming how users interact with social media. Platforms like Instagram, Snapchat, and TikTok have already integrated AR filters and effects, while VR-powered spaces like Meta's Horizon Worlds are redefining social experiences.

- **AR in Social Media:** Augmented reality overlays digital elements onto the real world. This technology is widely used in filters, virtual try-ons, and interactive shopping experiences.
- **VR in Social Media:** Virtual reality offers immersive experiences that transport users into digital environments. VR social platforms allow users to interact in virtual spaces, attend events, and explore branded worlds.

Why AR/VR Is the Future

The increasing adoption of AR/VR technologies is driven by advancements in hardware, 5G connectivity, and consumer demand for interactive experiences. For marketers, AR/VR represents a new frontier for engaging audiences in innovative and memorable ways.

- **Enhanced User Engagement:** AR/VR enables users to interact with content in ways that were previously impossible, fostering deeper connections with brands.
- **Immersive Shopping Experiences:** Virtual showrooms and AR-powered product try-ons make online shopping more engaging and personalized.
- **Event Marketing:** Virtual reality events and experiences can bring people together from around the world, creating unique opportunities for global outreach.

Strategies for Marketers

1. **Invest in AR-Driven Campaigns:** Develop AR filters, interactive ads, and virtual try-ons to provide engaging and practical experiences for users.
2. **Explore VR Platforms:** Experiment with VR spaces to host virtual events, launch products, or build branded experiences.
3. **Collaborate with Tech Partners:** Work with AR/VR developers to create high-quality, innovative content that aligns with your brand's goals.

Adapting to Disruptions and Staying Resilient

The Importance of Agility

The rapid pace of change in social media requires marketers to remain agile and adaptable. New platforms, regulations, and consumer preferences can disrupt existing strategies, but they also open doors to innovation.

Building Ethical Marketing Practices

As technology evolves, ethical considerations such as data privacy, accessibility, and inclusivity will become increasingly important. Brands that prioritize these values will not only stand out but also foster lasting relationships with their audiences.

Actionable Steps to Stay Future-Ready

1. **Monitor Emerging Trends:** Stay informed about new platforms, technologies, and consumer behaviors by subscribing to industry blogs, attending conferences, and participating in relevant online communities.
2. **Invest in Continuous Learning:** Equip your team with the skills and knowledge needed to adapt to new tools and strategies through training programs and certifications.
3. **Embrace Experimentation:** Dedicate resources to testing innovative campaigns on emerging platforms and technologies. Use data-driven insights to refine your approach.
4. **Focus on Sustainability:** Incorporate sustainability and inclusivity into your marketing strategy to resonate with socially conscious consumers.

5. **Collaborate with Innovators:** Partner with tech companies, creators, and influencers who are leading the way in adopting new technologies and trends.

Emerging trends like decentralized social media and AR/VR are reshaping the social media marketing landscape. By staying ahead of these innovations and adopting forward-thinking strategies, marketers can position their brands for long-term success. Preparing for the future isn't just about adapting to change—it's about embracing it as an opportunity to innovate and grow. The brands that thrive will be those that lead with creativity, authenticity, and a commitment to building meaningful connections in the digital age.

CHAPTER 16: Adapting to a Dynamic Digital Landscape

The digital landscape is constantly evolving, with new technologies, platforms, and user behaviors emerging at an unprecedented pace. As social media marketers, the key to long-term success lies in our ability to adapt quickly, anticipate change, and harness the power of innovation. In this chapter, we'll explore strategies to stay ahead of algorithm changes, leverage cutting-edge tools for continuous learning, and build resilience to thrive in an ever-changing environment.

How to Stay Ahead of Algorithm Changes

Understanding Social Media Algorithms

At the heart of social media platforms lies the algorithm—the set of rules and processes that determine which content appears in a user's feed. Algorithms are designed to deliver content that is most likely to engage users, based on their behaviors, preferences, and interactions. However, these algorithms are constantly evolving. What worked yesterday may not work today, and strategies that once drove high engagement may no longer have the same impact.

Why Algorithm Changes Matter

Platform algorithms have a direct impact on visibility and engagement. For businesses and marketers, staying ahead of algorithm changes is crucial for maintaining a strong online presence, reaching target audiences, and driving results.

- **Organic Reach Limitations:** Social platforms like Facebook, Instagram, and LinkedIn have been reducing organic reach, pushing businesses to rely on paid ads. Algorithms prioritize content that generates higher engagement, so understanding how to optimize your content for these changes is vital.
- **Emphasis on User Experience:** Algorithms increasingly prioritize content that promotes positive user experiences, such as engaging videos, relevant posts, and personalized recommendations. Understanding these preferences allows marketers to tailor content effectively.
- **Shift to Video Content:** Platforms like Instagram and TikTok prioritize video content in their algorithms, making it crucial to incorporate dynamic formats such as Reels, Stories, and TikToks to capture attention and foster engagement.

How to Stay Ahead of Algorithm Changes

1. **Monitor Platform Updates:** Stay informed about changes in algorithms by following social media news, official blog posts, and announcements from platforms. Many companies release details about algorithm adjustments, offering insight into their priorities.
2. **Test and Adapt Regularly:** Consistently test different types of content—images, videos, carousels,

and stories—to see what resonates with your audience. Use this data to refine your strategies.
3. **Leverage Engagement:** Encourage interaction by creating engaging content that fosters conversations, comments, and shares. Platforms reward content that drives higher user engagement.
4. **Build Relationships with Your Audience:** Invest in building authentic relationships with your audience by interacting in real time. Respond to comments, share user-generated content, and use personalized messaging to stay connected with followers.

Tools and Resources for Lifelong Learning

The Need for Lifelong Learning

The pace of digital transformation is rapid, and social media marketing is no exception. As a marketer, remaining relevant and competitive requires a commitment to continuous learning. New tools, platforms, and strategies emerge frequently, and the best way to stay ahead is to remain a student of the industry.

Lifelong learning ensures that you remain adaptable to changes in the digital space, empowering you to stay at the forefront of trends and technologies. It's not just about keeping up with changes—it's about anticipating them and leveraging new tools to unlock fresh opportunities.

Tools for Staying Up-to-Date

1. **Social Media Management Platforms:** Tools like Hootsuite, Buffer, and Sprout Social offer valuable insights into social media performance and keep you updated on trends in real-time.
2. **Analytics Tools:** Google Analytics, Facebook Insights, and platform-specific tools (e.g., Instagram Insights, YouTube Analytics) help you understand how your content is performing and offer data-driven recommendations.
3. **Industry News Sites:** Platforms like Social Media Examiner, HubSpot Blog, and Sprout Social's blog regularly publish updates and best practices for the latest developments in social media marketing.
4. **Online Courses and Certifications:** Invest in online learning platforms like Coursera, LinkedIn Learning, and Google Skillshop, where you can gain certifications in marketing tools, data analytics, and emerging trends like AR/VR and AI.
5. **Networking and Communities:** Join social media marketing communities, attend webinars, and participate in industry events to keep learning from peers, influencers, and thought leaders.

Developing a Lifelong Learning Mindset

1. **Commit to Regular Learning:** Dedicate a portion of your time each week to reading industry blogs, taking courses, and participating in webinars. Staying informed is essential for success in the fast-moving digital landscape.
2. **Embrace Experimentation:** Don't be afraid to try new tools, platforms, or strategies. Experiment with new features on Instagram, TikTok, or emerging platforms to discover what works for your brand.
3. **Participate in Peer Discussions:** Engage in conversations with fellow marketers to exchange tips, best practices, and lessons learned. Collaborating with others accelerates your growth.

Building Resilience for Long-Term Success

The Importance of Resilience in Marketing

Resilience is the ability to bounce back from setbacks, adapt to change, and keep moving forward. In the context of social media marketing, resilience means maintaining your brand's presence and performance even when algorithms change, platforms rise and fall, or marketing tactics evolve.

Adapting to change and staying committed to your long-term vision can help your brand navigate through disruptions while continuing to thrive. Here are the key components of building resilience for long-term social media marketing success:

1. Diversifying Your Strategy

Relying on one platform or marketing tactic is risky in a rapidly changing environment. A diversified strategy helps mitigate risks and ensures that your brand can withstand shifts in the digital landscape.

- **Platform Diversification:** Don't put all your eggs in one basket. Spread your marketing efforts across multiple platforms, including Facebook, Instagram, TikTok, LinkedIn, and emerging decentralized platforms. This allows your brand to reach different audiences and remain resilient when one platform undergoes changes.
- **Content Diversification:** Explore different types of content such as blogs, videos, podcasts, and infographics. Diversifying content ensures that your audience remains engaged regardless of algorithm changes.

2. Building a Brand That Stands for Something

Brands that have a clear purpose, values, and mission resonate deeply with their audience. In times of disruption, these values act as an anchor that keeps both the brand and its followers grounded. Whether your brand is focused on sustainability, innovation, or community, having a strong identity gives you the resilience to weather the storm.

- **Stand for Ethical Practices:** Consumers are increasingly looking to support brands that reflect their values. Being ethical, transparent, and socially responsible is essential for building long-term brand loyalty.
- **Consistency is Key:** Whether you're posting on social media, interacting with your community, or running ad campaigns, maintaining a consistent message and tone builds trust and encourages lasting relationships with your audience.

3. Cultivating an Innovative Mindset

A forward-thinking mindset enables you to stay ahead of trends, embrace new technologies, and spot opportunities that others may overlook. This mindset encourages continuous improvement and adaptation.

- **Embrace Change:** Be open to new technologies, like AR/VR, blockchain, and AI. The brands that succeed in the future will be the ones that embrace innovation rather than shy away from it.
- **Foster Creativity:** Encourage your team to think outside the box and try new approaches to engagement. Creativity fuels innovation and helps brands differentiate themselves in a crowded market.

4. Building Long-Term Relationships with Customers

Resilience also comes from the relationships you build with your audience. Brands that foster strong, lasting relationships with their customers are better able to adapt to changes because they have a loyal community that supports them through thick and thin.

- **Community Engagement:** Engage with your audience regularly, ask for feedback, and create opportunities for two-way communication. When your audience feels heard, they are more likely to stick with you through changes.
- **Personalized Experiences:** Use data to deliver personalized experiences to your audience. People want to feel that brands understand their needs, and personalized communication builds trust and loyalty.

Actionable Steps for Staying Future-Ready

1. **Stay Updated with Emerging Trends:** Continuously monitor new platforms, technologies, and trends that could impact your industry. Embrace new opportunities and innovate your marketing strategy.
2. **Emphasize Data-Driven Decisions:** Use data analytics to inform your decisions. Monitor trends, track KPIs, and analyze customer behaviors to adjust your strategy accordingly.
3. **Foster a Growth Mindset:** Cultivate an environment where learning, testing, and improving is the norm. Stay curious, be willing to pivot, and continuously invest in your development.

4. **Resilience Through Relationships:** Build deep, meaningful relationships with your customers. By maintaining strong connections, your brand will be more resilient to changes and challenges in the digital space.

To succeed in the rapidly evolving world of social media marketing, adaptability is key. By staying ahead of algorithm changes, embracing continuous learning, and building resilience, you can ensure that your brand remains relevant and successful in the face of disruptions. The future of social media marketing is full of opportunity, and by staying future-ready, you'll be able to navigate the digital landscape with confidence, agility, and innovation.

CONCLUSION

Turning Magic Into Mastery

As we come to the end of this journey through the dynamic world of social media marketing, it's time to reflect on the powerful insights we've uncovered and how to transform them into lasting success. The world of social media is ever-changing, and mastering it requires not just understanding the tools and strategies at hand, but also the magic of creativity, adaptability, and innovation.

Recap of Key Insights and Takeaways

Throughout this book, we've explored the building blocks of social media marketing, from defining clear goals and crafting a compelling brand identity to leveraging the latest trends and technologies. Here are the key takeaways that will serve as your foundation for success:

1. **Setting Clear Goals:** Every successful social media strategy begins with clear, measurable goals. Whether you're aiming for brand awareness, increased engagement, or lead generation, aligning your social media efforts with your broader business objectives ensures that every post, ad, and interaction serves a purpose.

2. **Building a Strong Brand Identity:** The power of storytelling, a consistent visual presence, and trust-building in a digital world cannot be overstated. Establishing a brand that speaks to your audience's values and needs is key to creating meaningful relationships that last.
3. **Engaging Content Creation:** From storytelling to interactive formats like AR and polls, creating engaging content that resonates with your audience is a vital ingredient in your social media success. Content that encourages shares, conversations, and emotional connections will set you apart in a crowded digital landscape.
4. **Platform-Specific Strategies:** Every platform has its unique strengths, audience demographics, and best practices. Understanding how to tailor your approach for platforms like Facebook, Instagram, TikTok, and others ensures that your content stands out in the right places and reaches the right people.
5. **Leveraging Data and Analytics:** Data-driven decision-making is essential for continuous growth. By using the right analytics tools and A/B testing strategies, you can optimize your campaigns, refine your content, and measure what's working to maximize your ROI.
6. **Embracing Innovation and Adaptability:** From AI-driven tools to emerging trends like decentralized social media, staying ahead of technological advancements and adapting to changes ensures that your strategies remain fresh and effective in a fast-paced digital world.

Applying the Magic to Your Brand

Now that you have the tools, strategies, and insights needed to succeed in the social media marketing space, it's time to turn the magic into mastery. Social media is no longer just about posting content—it's about crafting experiences, building communities, and driving meaningful engagement. The magic comes when you blend creativity with data, innovation with consistency, and strategy with adaptability.

Here's your call to action: Take the insights you've gained from this book and apply them to your brand. Start by setting clear, actionable goals that align with your overall business strategy. Develop content that resonates with your audience's values and interests, and don't be afraid to experiment with new formats and technologies. Whether you're crafting a compelling video, running a targeted ad campaign, or experimenting with an emerging platform, stay focused on delivering value to your audience.

Encouragement to Innovate, Adapt, and Lead

The future of social media marketing is full of opportunities for those who are willing to innovate, adapt, and lead. Change is inevitable, but rather than seeing it as a challenge, view it as an opportunity to push the boundaries of what's possible. The brands that succeed in the future will be the ones that are not afraid to evolve, experiment, and take risks.

As you move forward, keep pushing the envelope. Stay curious and open to learning new tools, strategies, and platforms. Build resilience in your brand by focusing on long-term relationships with your audience, staying ahead of trends, and embracing new technologies. Most importantly, lead with authenticity and purpose. Your brand's uniqueness and values are what will set you apart in a sea of competition.

Social media marketing is both an art and a science—a blend of creativity, strategy, and data-driven decision-making. By mastering the fundamentals and embracing the future of digital marketing, you can turn the magic of social media into real business success. The digital landscape is yours to conquer. Now, go ahead and create something extraordinary. Your brand's future starts today.

A Note to My Readers

Thank you for taking the time to read *this book*. I hope this book has provided you with valuable insights and practical strategies to elevate your online presence and achieve your marketing goals.

If you found this book helpful, I would truly appreciate it if you could take a moment to leave a review and rating on Amazon. Your feedback not only helps other readers discover this book but also allows me to continue creating content that serves your needs.

Every review makes a difference, and I'd love to hear your thoughts!

Thank you for your support, and I wish you great success in your social media marketing journey.

Medina Fred

www.ingramcontent.com/pod-product-compliance
Lightning Source LLC
Chambersburg PA
CBHW052206220526
45471CB00004B/1841